DAVID TAYLOR

111 PLACES IN THE YORKSHIRE DALES THAT YOU SHOULDN'T MISS

111

emons:

MIX
Paper | Supporting responsible forestry
FSC® C177064
FSC www.fsc.org

Cäcilienstraße 48, 50667 Köln
info@emons-verlag.de

Layout: Anja Sauerland, based on a design by Lübbeke | Naumann | Thoben
Maps: altancicek.design, www.altancicek.de
Basic cartographical information from Openstreetmap,
© OpenStreetMap-Mitwirkende, OdbL
QR code notice: External content is provided via Google Maps.
Google's privacy policy applies.
Edited by Ros Horton
Printing and binding: sourc-e GmbH
Printed in Europe 2026
ISBN 978-3-7408-2792-2

FOREWORD

The Yorkshire Dales lie at the heart of 'God's Own County'. They are a wonderful mix of soft rolling hills and rugged open moorland, and of bustling market towns and charming villages. This is a land celebrated in best-selling literature as well as being the pleasing backdrop to many beloved movies and television shows.

There is no hard border that defines the *exact* area that everyone knows as the Yorkshire Dales. They're not even entirely in Yorkshire! The eponymous national park leaks ever so slightly into the neighbouring counties of Cumbria and Lancashire. (That can be our little secret, however.) For the purposes of this book the Yorkshire Dales include the national park, the wonderful if overlooked Nidderdale National Landscape, as well as the major towns that lurk at the edge of the Dales, such as Harrogate and Ilkley.

One theme running through this book is how important geology is in defining the character of the Dales. There are cave systems to explore, thrusting scars to wonder at, and limestone pavements to pick a careful way across. The landscape also inspired scientists such as Adam Sedgwick, as well as artists like J. M. W. Turner.

Choosing which places to include in the book was agonising. There sadly wasn't room to fit in everything that you could possibly see or do in the Dales! Some of the places in the following pages were unmissable, however. The charismatic three peaks that are Whernside, Ingleborough, Pen-y-ghent had to be included, as did other natural wonders such as Malham Tarn and Cautley Spout. And then there are places that were included for the simple reason that I like them. The wonderfully eccentric Forbidden Corner and Billy Bob's Parlour fall into this category. Whether you're a visitor or actually live in the Dales, I hope this book inspires you to thoroughly explore this captivating corner of the British Isles.

FAVOURITE TOURS

The Yorkshire Dales are wonderfully varied, with something for everyone. There are numerous public footpaths that crisscross the landscape, so you won't be short of places to walk if you want to stretch your legs. Cycling is a great way to explore a particular dale, though be prepared for a strenuous day if your chosen route takes you over a pass between two dales.

A MAGICAL HISTORY TOUR

People have lived in the Yorkshire Dales for millennia. This drive will take you to places where our ancestors left a tangible architectural mark. Start at Kirkby Stephen's parish church to see the mysterious Loki Stone ch. 23, a representation of a Norse god with a liking for practical jokes. Head south towards Mallerstang but be sure to stop at Pendragon Castle ch. 25 where King Arthur's dad supposedly lived (spoilers, he didn't). Continue on to Hawes and the Dales Countryside Museum ch. 79, a truly fascinating place where you can learn about farming, lead mining and life in the Dales in centuries past. From Hawes it's only a short hop to Aysgarth and the Edwardian Rock Garden ch. 80, the creation of local eccentric Frank Sayer-Graham and lovingly restored earlier this century. Next, head to Holy Trinity Church ch. 82 in Wensley. This wonderful building houses striking examples of 16th-century wood carving – the animal-themed pew ends are a particular treat. Wensley itself ch. 87 is something of a curiosity. It was once the most important community in Wensleydale but declined after an outbreak of the plague. From Wensley drive to the village of Middleham to take a walk around Middleham Castle ch. 84. This ruined structure was the childhood home of Richard III, one of England's more… problematic kings. Finally, continue on to Jervaulx Abbey ch. 83. Now ruined, the abbey was once the home of Cistercian monks until dissolved by Henry VIII.

VILLAGES AND TOWNS

There are many wonderful villages and towns in the Yorkshire Dales, each with their own unique character. This tour takes you along Wharfedale and into Nidderdale. Start at the charming hamlet of Hubberholme ch. 92, a favourite spot of playwright J. B. Priestley and where his ashes were buried. Head south from there to Starbotton ch. 95, a quiet village with an abundance of interesting stories from history. From there continue on to Kettlewell ch. 105 and take a walk along the Wharfe. If you visit Kettlewell at the right time of year you can also experience the eccentric and fun Scarecrow Festival ch. 94. From Kettlewell drive to Grassington ch. 90, which is the face of the fictional village of Darrowby in the modern TV version of James Herriot's *All Creatures Great and Small*. Next, head east to Pateley Bridge and the Oldest Sweetshop in the World ch. 35, where you can stock up on traditional sweets made the old-fashioned way. End your journey in the town of Harrogate, where you can reward yourself with a splendid meal at the Caffé Lago di Como ch. 13, or learn more about how Harrogate became a spa town at the Old Magnesia Well Pump Room ch. 14.

SPLENDID VIEWS

There's no denying that the Dales are fabulously beautiful, whatever the weather or the time of year. This driving route takes you past some of the most spectacular sights in the region. Start at Ribblehead Viaduct ch. 2, an architectural and engineering masterpiece. To the north is Whernside ch. 4 the highest hill in the Dales and to the south is Ingleborough ch. 1, arguably the most handsome. Leave Ribblehead and take the road towards Horton-in-Ribblesdale. You'll soon see the brooding shape of Pen-y-ghent ch. 46, a curiously named peak on the route of the Pennine Way. At Langcliffe take the road towards Malham. Park at Malham and take the path to the wonder that is Malham Cove ch. 29. Finish off the tour by visiting the majestic Gordale Scar ch. 28.

111 PLACES

Scan here for
the digital map

1 Ingleborough

One down, two to go

Beauty is in the eye of the beholder, of course. But is there another hill in the Yorkshire Dales – in the whole of Yorkshire for that matter – that is as ruggedly handsome as Ingleborough? It is an eminence 2,372 feet in height with a variety of routes to the top, some of which are harder and more physically challenging than others (though none are a pushover). Alfred Wainwright, the best-selling author of walking guides to the fells of Cumbria and Yorkshire, thought that the path from Clapham, via Trow Gill, was one of the finest walks in the Dales.

There is evidence the Brigantes tribe settled on Ingleborough; the fractured remains of an Iron-Age fort, built in the first century A.D., can (just about) be seen on Ingleborough's plateau.

Ingleborough is the second highest peak in the Yorkshire Dales and is, along with Pen-y-ghent and Whernside, one of the 'Three Peaks'. If you're fit and up for a challenge then the Three Peaks Circular is for you. This is a 24-mile walk that takes you to the summit of all three hills, and involves over 5,000 feet of climbing in total. The route starts in Horton-in-Ribblesdale with Pen-y-ghent, the most easterly of the three hills, first on the list. Whernside, the most northerly peak and arguably the least interesting, is tackled next. Perhaps fittingly, Ingleborough is the final peak on the walk, though a good dollop of mental fortitude is required to keep yourself going all the way to the top. There is some comfort to be had, though, from the welcome fact that it's all downhill back to Horton-in-Ribblesdale and the starting line.

Depending on your level of fitness, the Three Peaks Circular should take about 12 hours to complete. If you really want to push yourself though, you could try to beat the record set by Andy Peace in 1996. Andy completed the current Three Peaks Circular route in a truly stupefying 2 hours, 46 minutes and 3 seconds.

ADDRESS The summit of Ingleborough is marked by an OS trig point at ghosts.prospered.dispenser TIP If you want to see *under* Ingleborough then take the fascinating tour of White Scar Cave, the longest show cave in Britain (www.whitescarcave.co.uk).

2 Ribblehead Viaduct

Saved for the nation

Ribblehead Viaduct is an engineering wonder. The sturdy structure has carried passengers and freight on the Settle–Carlisle railway line since 1876. Designed by John Sydney Crossley, the viaduct boasts 24 spans and is the longest structure on the line.

The construction of Ribblehead Viaduct was dramatised by ITV in 2016. The eight-part series *Jericho* tells the story of the recently widowed Annie (Jessica Raine), who travels to the eponymous shanty town with her children to start a new life. There she encounters the men (and women) who are working on the viaduct – renamed Culverdale for the series. After a number of adventures, Annie gets to see the structure slowly rise up from the surrounding moorland. Although perhaps a touch overly dramatic at times (it plays more like a Western set in Yorkshire), the series is – at least until time travel is invented – the simplest way to get a flavour of what life was like for the navvies who built the viaduct.

Ribblehead Viaduct has had its problems over the years. On 9 December, 1964, the *Birmingham Post* reported that the viaduct was closed as 'gale-force winds had dislodged seven cars on a freight train'. The accident blocked the line for almost five hours and caused delays to trains further afield.

However, the viaduct faced its greatest test in the 1980s when British Railways threatened to close the Settle–Carlisle line. After more than a century of use, the viaduct looked to be in need of some *very* expensive repair work. Happily, thanks to a decision by the then Minister of Transport, the line was saved due to its status as an example of Victorian engineering. In 1990, the Settle & Carlisle Railway Trust was established to maintain the line, and the necessary (and far cheaper-than-expected) repairs carried out on Ribblehead Viaduct. The line is now a popular attraction, with the view from the viaduct being one of its many highlights.

ADDRESS Ingleton, Chapel-le-Dale, LA6 3AU, North Yorkshire, robes.cups.ramp
TIP Ribblehead Station is strangely lopsided. The original northbound platform was demolished in 1970 so that sidings for a nearby quarry could be built.

3 St Leonard's Church

Journey's end

On 17 August, 1876, a lengthy article was published in *The Sheffield and Rotherham Independent.* Headlined 'The New Route to Scotland', the piece is a detailed account of a journey on the then newly opened Settle–Carlisle Railway. Out on a 'wild moorland wilderness' near 'where the Ribble takes its rise on the slopes of Cam Fell', the writer spots 'a town of a most extraordinary description'. This was Batty Green, a cluster of wooden shanty houses built for the navvies who constructed Ribblehead Viaduct and Blea Tunnel. 'Some two thousand of these brawny-armed sons of toil were located at Batty Green' notes the author admiringly, mentioning also that the 'work these men had to do was of no ordinary kind'. This was something of an understatement.

Batty Green was actually a collection of nine camps, three of which were named Batty Wife Hole, Sebastopol and Belgravia. The timber buildings are long gone, though earthworks are still visible. Batty Green was named after Batty Moss, the stretch of moorland over which Ribblehead Viaduct crosses, and the area is still shown on OS Explorer maps.

Hundreds of navvies lost their lives during the building of the Settle–Carlisle Railway. The deaths were mainly due to accidents, though smallpox was also a significant factor. The stretch of railway from Batty Moss to Blea Moor tunnel was a particularly dangerous place to work. So many men were killed there that the owners of Midland Railway paid to increase the size of the churchyard at St Leonard's Church in nearby Chapel-le-Dale. In total, some two hundred men, women and children were buried there between 1870 and 1877. Some of these graves can still be seen today, as can two poignant memorials, one inside the church, the other – raised in the year 2000 – out in the churchyard. All are a sobering reminder of the heavy price that is often paid for progress.

ADDRESS Chapel-le-Dale, LA6 3AR, North Yorkshire, discusses.plenty.enhanced
TIP Look out for butterflies fluttering around Southerscales Nature Reserve (jiffy.cure.overused) during the spring and summer months.

4 Whernside

None higher

None of the hills in the Yorkshire Dales are particularly high as these things go. Whernside is the loftiest peak in the region but the summit is 'only' 2,415 feet above sea level. That sounds impressive until you discover that Whernside is a lowly 84th on the list of peaks in England ordered by height, and 1,476th on a similar list for the United Kingdom.

One consolation for fans of Whernside is that it is a Nuttall, the name given to a peak in England or Wales over 2,000 feet in height (Scotland has its own naming system). The honour was bestowed by Anne and John Nuttall in their comprehensive two-volume book *The Mountains of England and Wales*, first published in 1990. Fittingly, John and Anne were the first to summit all 442 Nuttalls. James Forrest currently holds the record for completing the Nuttalls in the shortest possible time. He managed this feat in 2017, having taken a mere six months from the first to the last.

Whernside is one of the 'Three Peaks'. Compared with Ingleborough and Pen-y-ghent, Whernside is *relatively* easy to climb, though only for those with a good level of fitness. You can make it hard for yourself by taking the steep path from Bruntscar. However, most sensible people follow the considerably longer but more gently sloped path from Ribblehead.

Just like Ingleborough and Pen-y-ghent, the main bulk of Whernside is limestone capped by a plateau of millstone grit. The latter is a coarse-grained sandstone laid down during the Carboniferous some 358 to 298 million years ago (a period when the world's coal reserves were forming and amphibians evolved). Millstone grit was once used to make the grinding stones found in watermills, hence the name. Unlike Ingleborough and Pen-y-ghent, there are tarns on the Whernside plateau, 'tarn' being the northern word for a mountain pool.

ADDRESS The summit of Whernside is marked by an OS trig point at cooked. mount.pools **TIP** Quench your thirst after your walk at the Station Inn at Ribblehead, where you can get a pint or a hot meal (www.thestationinnribblehead.com).

5 Gaping Gill

'I give you the centre of the Earth!'

Gaping Gill is a superlative natural wonder, though not one that is easily seen. It is an enormous underground chamber roughly 100 feet high, 423 feet long and 82 feet wide, a (literally) cavernous space into which York Minster could snugly fit. The entrance to the cave is an unfenced vertical shaft – the edge of which you *really* shouldn't go near – on the slopes of Ingleborough. Fell Beck flows into this Stygian pit, tumbling 330 feet straight down, making it England's highest unbroken waterfall.

Fortunately, there *is* a way to safely explore Gaping Gill. This is during a public 'winch meet', held twice a year by volunteers from the Bradford and Craven pothole clubs. As the name suggests, this is an opportunity to be winched down into Gaping Gill. Tickets are booked online and quickly sell out.

On winch day you first make your way to Gaping Gill from the village of Clapham. The first indication that you're close is a cluster of tents. This temporary canvas village is where the volunteers live for two weeks. Once you've checked in you then wait your turn with your fellow explorers. When your name is called you are directed to a sturdy platform erected over what you can now see is a vastly deep and dark hole. A guide directs you to sit in a very snug cage and straps you in firmly. You then begin your descent.

The journey to the bottom of the Gaping Gill is remarkably swift. You first drop through a narrow gap known as a chimney before the cave suddenly opens out beneath you. The clubs thoughtfully light the cave on winch days so you can quickly appreciate the scale of the space below your feet. And then all too soon the floor of the cave rushes towards you and you safely come to a stop. Experienced hands quickly and efficiently release you and you are then free to explore the cave on your own. Once you've satisfied your curiosity, all that remains is to join the queue for the journey back up.

ADDRESS Clapham, LA2 8EE, North Yorkshire, www.bpc-cave.org.uk or www.cravenpotholeclub.org, risks.cheer.hiker **TIP** Ingleborough Cave is an easier and far less nerve-shredding way to see an Ingleborough cave system (www.ingleboroughcave.co.uk).

6 The Forbidden Corner

'Curiouser and curiouser!'

A lot happened in 1974. It was the year the Soviet Russian car firm Lada started selling cars in Britain; Brian Clough spent a fraught 44 days managing Leeds United before being sacked; Jon Pertwee regenerated into Tom Baker in the TV series *Doctor Who*; and China graciously donated two giant pandas to London Zoo. It was also the year that Colin Armstrong bought Tupgill Park – his childhood home – and decided to restore the stables on the estate.

That simple decision resulted in the planting of fir trees to act as a windbreak. Several years, and three children, later, Colin, with his gardener Doug Weatherill, created a grass maze for the family's amusement. More years passed and then it was decided that a secluded bower should be built. In 1989 Malcolm Tempest, a friend and architect, suggested building a wall to protect the bower. That led to the notion of creating a grotto. Despite the cost and complexity of doing this, Colin decided that a grotto was a capital idea and so it was done. Things snowballed at that point. Mature students at Hull University got in touch asking to see the work-in-progress. And so, in July 1993, Colin's nascent wonderland had its very first visitors. Happily, they were utterly enchanted by what they saw. Perhaps, thought Colin at this point, the general public should be invited in to see what he, his family and friends were creating.

Today, The Forbidden Corner welcomes visitors from around the globe. It is the self-styled 'Strangest Place in the World', which isn't *too* much of an exaggeration. What other attraction has you enter via a giant burping mouth? Or a labyrinth, at the heart of which is a spooky fountain? As well as any number of talking mice, card-playing bears and a huge green man? There is so much to see (and so many different ways of getting lost) that it's all too easy to miss something. But, is that such a bad thing? It's an excuse to make a second visit. And perhaps even a third or fourth...

ADDRESS Tupgill Park Estate, Middleham, Leyburn, North Yorkshire, DL8 4TJ, +44 (0)1969 640638, www.theforbiddencorner.co.uk **TIP** Just a few minutes' drive from The Forbidden Corner, Pinker's Pond is a great place to see various species of waterfowl (unearthly.trusts.costly).

7 Adam Sedgwick Memorial

Geological column

Many singular men and women have been born in Yorkshire. The village of Dent can boast the geologist Adam Sedgwick as one of their own. Sedgwick was born on 22 March, 1785, the third child of Revd Richard Sedgwick and his wife Margaret. The young Sedgwick was keenly interested in nature, and collected fossils and rocks. He was educated at Sedbergh School, before entering Trinity College, Cambridge as a scholarship student. In 1818 he became the Woodwardian Professor of Geology at Cambridge.

Sedgwick is now best known for proposing and then naming the Cambrian, the first geological period of the Palaeozoic era. The Cambrian began some 538 million years ago and lasted just over 50 million years. It was during this period that complex multi-cellular life proliferated in the Earth's seas, leaving a mark in the fossil record that Sedgwick would later discover and interpret.

Another contribution to science was choosing Charles Darwin as a field assistant in 1831. Darwin accompanied Sedgwick to north Wales where the two examined the local rocks. This gave Darwin useful experience in field geology that was put to good use during his voyage on HMS *Beagle*. The two remained friends until Sedgwick's death in 1873 despite Darwin's proposal that life evolved over time by natural selection, a notion that Sedgwick, as a Christian, thought contradicted the idea of a divine creator. In a letter to Darwin in 1859, written after reading *On the Origin of Species*, Sedgwick wrote 'I have read your book with more pain than pleasure. Parts of it I admired greatly; parts I laughed at till my sides were almost sore; other parts I read with absolute sorrow'.

Dent's memorial to Adam Sedgwick was erected in the late 19th century. Made from roughly-dressed pink granite, the angular memorial also sports a fountain and trough. Until the 1920s, this was the village's only source of drinkable water.

ADDRESS Main Street, Dent, LA10 5QL, North Yorkshire, www.yorkshiredales.org.uk
TIP St Andrew's Church in the village boasts distinctive floor tiles made from Dent 'marble', a dark limestone that was quarried locally for more than three centuries.

8 Dent Station

Be prepared for a walk

In all sorts of ways, the Yorkshire Dales are the last place you'd want to build a railway through. Trains are most efficient on flat ground and the Yorkshire Dales are very definitely not flat. The Victorian engineers who were commissioned to build the Settle–Carlisle line must have wondered what they'd let themselves in for. Fortunately, they succeeded in creating a railway line that is arguably one of the most scenic and thrilling in England.

Despite their best efforts, the men who designed and built the line inevitably had to make the occasional compromise here or there. One of these concessions to topography is Dent railway station, which is some five miles from and 400 feet higher than the village it serves. This is more than inconvenient for the good people of Dent of course, but it has resulted in a wonderfully quirky and record-breaking railway station.

Dent railway station opened on 6 August, 1877. It was placed neatly between Blea Moor Tunnel and Arten Gill Viaduct to the south and Rise Hill Tunnel to the north. Situated at an altitude of 1,150 feet, it is England's highest operational station on the National Rail network (beaten only by Corrour in Scotland).

Look carefully on the hillside behind the station and you can see what look like sturdy fences made from railway sleepers. These are snow fences built to prevent snow rolling down the slope onto the track, a once necessary feature thanks to the station's height above sea level. A photo of a snowbound Dent railway station in *The Yorkshire Observer* on 3 March, 1947 shows that heavy winters could still occasionally close the line, despite this protection.

Dent railway station was closed in 1970, but was re-opened by British Rail in 1986. If you're travelling on the Settle–Carlisle line do consider alighting at Dent. It may be a long walk to anywhere but that's not the point. It is a destination in its own right.

ADDRESS Coal Road, Dent, LA10 5RF, North Yorkshire, +44 (0)1768 351311, www.settle-carlisle.co.uk **TIP** The handsome Arten Gill Viaduct, two miles south-east of Dent Station, featured in the movie *Miss Potter* starring Renée Zellweger.

9 Flintergill Wishing Tree

Riches? A long life? You decide

It's a short but steep walk from the village of Dent to the Flintergill Wishing Tree. However, it is worth the effort, for a visit to this particular arboreal marvel will change your life. Possibly. The tree is an oak that at some exciting point in the past had the earth bank on which it stands washed away. The event exposed the tree's root structure and created a gnarled and knotty natural arch that can – with care not to bump your head! – be passed under.

Local lore has it that the spirit of the tree will grant you a wish if you pass under the arch three times in a 'deiseal' (clockwise) direction. Take care though. Bad luck will soon follow if you circle the tree in a widdershins (anti-clockwise) direction. Widdershins is a wonderfully evocative word commonly used in lowland Scotland. It describes the act of moving around an object so that the object is always on your left. This is contrary to the way that the sun appears to move across the sky in the Northern Hemisphere.

Trees have long been associated with wishes, spirituality or the granting of good luck. In recognition of such sterling service, trees are often left votive offerings. This sometimes takes the form of coins hammered into the trunk, a practice now frowned upon as it does the poor tree no good at all. More socially acceptable is the pressing of coins into fallen trees. You can see such trees at Bolton Abbey and on the Ingleton Waterfalls Trail.

Another (Scottish) tradition is the clootie tree – typically ash or hawthorn – found growing next to a holy well. Strips of cloth would first be dipped in the water of the well before being tied to the branches of the tree. This was believed to cure illness; the ailment was thought to fade as the cloth disintegrated.

The Flintergill Wishing Tree does not need payment of any kind. No one would think less of you, though, if you want to give the roots a good old hug before you head back down to Dent.

ADDRESS Dent, LA10 5QR, North Yorkshire, www.yorkshiredales.org.uk **TIP** Not far from the tree are the 'Dancing Flags', flat blocks of limestone on which the 'Terrible Knitters of Dent' laid out fabric to make a kind of felt.

10 The Terrible Knitters of Dent

Purls of wisdom

Would you want to be described as terrible? It sounds like a horribly cutting insult, does it not? However, the word terrible was once used to describe a person (or object) likely to cause a strong feeling of dread or excitement, and not something bad or awful. This helps to explain the puzzling phrase 'The Terrible Knitters of Dent', who weren't hopeless at knitting at all. Far from it.

Three centuries ago everyone in Dent knitted: men, women and children. Life was hard in the Dales and so the extra income from selling knitted goods was an important supplement to a family's finances. It's said that men knitted as they walked to and from their place of work, and that women would pick up their needles once the housework was done. Neighbours would also gather together in one house after dark to share the warmth and light of a fire, chatting and singing as they knitted. In the warmer months, villagers would sit on their doorsteps and knit until the light finally faded.

Dent folk had a well-deserved reputation for their astonishing speed and dexterity, and for the quality of their work. A cunning wooden sheath known as a stick even allowed a knitter to knit with one hand, leaving the other hand free for another task. There were two types of yarn commonly used. A thick (and slightly) greasy wool was known as 'bump' and was reserved for heavy garments, whereas finer wool was used for more delicate products such as gloves.

The knitters of Dent were awarded their descriptive name in a story written by Robert Southey, in 1834. In the account, Southey tells the true tale of Betty and Sally Yewdale, who were sent to Dent in the 1760s to learn how to knit. Southey wrote in approving terms that 'they er terrible knitters e' Dent' and the name stuck. Find out far more about Dent's knitting tradition at the delightful Dent Village Museum and Heritage Centre.

ADDRESS Dent Village Museum and Heritage Centre, Laning, Dent, North Yorkshire, LA10 5QJ, +44 (0)1539 625800, www.dentvillageheritagecentre.com **TIP** Leave the pressures of the modern world behind at the Meditation Centre in Dent (www.meditationcentre.co.uk).

11 The Vampire Stone

You can't keep a good man down

A vampire is an undead creature who consumes the blood of humans, usually by piercing the neck of their victim with long and very pointed upper canine teeth. The one vampire most people have heard of is Count Dracula, the creation of Irish writer Bram Stoker. *Dracula* was published in 1897 and was a sensation. Since then, the novel has been adapted numerous times for stage, screen and television. Arguably the most celebrated portrayal of the count was that by Bela Lugosi, who played the titular character in a movie adaptation in 1931. Lugosi was so associated with the role that he was buried in a Dracula cape after his death in 1956.

Less well known is George Hodgson, referred to locally as the Vampire of Dent. George was born in 1621 and lived a remarkably long life for the time. When he died in 1715 he was laid to rest in a corner of St Andrew's churchyard. It was then that tales about George's eccentric lifestyle began to circulate. Gossips talked of his peculiar habit of drinking a daily glass of sheep's blood, and that this bizarre beverage explained George's curious longevity. And then there was the story of the farmer who shot at – but failed to kill – an unusual black hare. Injured, the animal slunk away but the farmer was able to follow its bloody trail. He soon arrived at George's cottage. Peering through a window, the farmer saw George attending to a fresh shotgun wound to his leg.

Perhaps it was these unsettling tales that prompted villagers to dig up George's coffin. To their understandable dismay, they discovered that George's body was uncorrupted and that his hair and fingernails had continued to grow. In a state of panic, the villagers moved George to a new grave outside the door of St Andrew's. To ensure that George stayed put, a slab was laid over the grave and a brass stake driven down through the stone. It must have worked because George has remained there ever since.

ADDRESS St Andrew's Church, Main Street, Dent, North Yorkshire, LA10 5QL, www.westerndales.org.uk TIP Wholesome food and drink can be had all day at the nearby Stone Close Tea Room (www.stoneclose.com).

12 Ruswarp

Faithful to the end

Graham Nuttall was a rail enthusiast and a staunch defender of the Settle–Carlisle railway line when it faced closure in the 1980s. He showed his determination by co-founding the Friends of the Settle–Carlisle Line, which aimed to raise awareness of the potential loss. One petition organised by the Friends collected more than 32,000 signatures. On 11 April, 1989, thanks to the work of Graham and other passionate like-minded folk, it was officially announced that the line was saved.

Graham was a keen walker and was often out on the hills in the company of his dog, Ruswarp (pronounced 'russup'), a 14-year-old Border Collie. On 20 January, 1990, Graham and Ruswarp set off from their home in Burnley for Llandrindod to go hiking in the Welsh hills. Neither returned home that night. Searchers combed the area thoroughly but neither man nor dog were found.

On 7 April, a walker came across the body of Graham next to a mountain stream. Ruswarp was there too. He had not left his master in all that time. Weak and painfully thin, the devoted dog had to be carried down the hill by his rescuers. Happily, a vet was able to nurse Ruswarp back to health and he was well enough to attend Graham's funeral. It was noted by one attendee that Ruswarp was quiet throughout the service until Graham's coffin slid behind the crematorium's curtain. It was only then that Ruswarp let out a deep and desperately sad howl.

For his dedication, Ruswarp was awarded the RSPCA's Medallion and Collar for Vigilance, as well as the Animal Plaque for Intelligence and Courage. Sadly, an already old dog, Ruswarp did not live for long after Graham's funeral. A handsome bronze sculpture of Ruswarp by Joel Walker was unveiled in 2009 at Garsdale Station. He looks across the southbound platform towards a bench on the other platform dedicated to Graham.

ADDRESS Garsdale Station, Coal Road, Garsdale Head, Cumbria, LA10 5PP, +44 (0)1768 351311, www.settle-carlisle.co.uk **TIP** Less than five miles east of Garsdale Station, Cotter Force is a very accessible waterfall where you may spot birds such as dippers and kingfishers.

13 Caffé Lago di Como

Molto gustoso!

Nertil Xhallo and Daniela Genova both had a dream. The two once worked as managers at the Saranda Bar and Grill in Harrogate. However, what they really wanted to do was open and run a jointly owned café. That opportunity soon came along.

The Caffé Lago di Como is an independent Italian café and bakery established by chef Antonio Cavinato in 2018. Four years later the business was for sale and Daniela and Nertil decided there and then to take it on. And so, with new and enthusiastic owners, the Caffé Lago di Como re-opened on Christmas Eve, 2022.

Nertil and Daniela work extremely hard to provide a tempting range of Italian dishes – both savoury and sweet and all made using their own recipes (10 different ready-to-eat meals and 10 or so types of cakes). They also bake focaccia breads that customers can take away. And all the food is freshly made on site by the two owners, seven days a week.

The pair are both experts in French wines and both have been finalists in the Lavazza competition for baristas (Daniela in Turin, Nertil in London). Their culinary skills are just one of their numerous talents, however. Nertil is a qualified architect who holds a Master's degree in the subject; Daniela was a semi-professional football player in Greece.

The interior of the Caffé Lago di Como has an appealing vintage feel, and Daniela and Nertil warmly welcome customers. It works. Sixty per cent of patrons are regulars (the other 40 per cent are probably just regulars-to-be making their first visit). The favourite savoury provided by the pair is their handmade Sicilian arancini. These are balls of arborio rice and a meat or cheese filling that are coated with breadcrumbs and deep-fried. If you've still got room after one (or two) of those then you really should try a slice of their pistachio cake, the most popular sweet treat with patrons.

ADDRESS 35 Beulah Street, Harrogate, North Yorkshire, HG1 1QH, www.cafelagodicomohg.com TIP The Old Swan Hotel in Harrogate is infamous as the place Agatha Christie reappeared after vanishing for 11 days in late 1926, claiming no knowledge of where she'd been during that time.

14 Old Magnesia Well Pump Room

Sulphur so good

Imagine that you were alive in the 19th century and that you suffered from a variety of ailments; just for fun, let's say gout and a niggling digestive disorder. There is no NHS and you (sensibly for the time) have a deep and abiding distrust of doctors. What do you do? One solution is to head to a spa town to take the waters. If you live in Yorkshire then Harrogate is the obvious choice. This is a town that owes its existence to the discovery of its medicinal mineral springs. It was once hailed as *the* English spa town, and its waters were recommended by no less a figure than the personal physician to Elizabeth I, Timothie Bright.

In 1571, a William Slingsby drank water from a well in Knaresborough Forest. The well was (and still is) a chalybeate source denoting that its water contains traces of iron. Slingsby had the notion that the water from the well reminded him of that from Spa, a town in Belgium. The well, now known as Tewit Well, can be found on the edge of the Stray in Harrogate.

Harrogate grew in size and popularity over the next 300 years as other springs were discovered. These included St John's Well (or Sweet Spa), found in 1631 by Dr Michael Stanhope. In his book, *Cures without Care*, Stanhope wrote of patients who had been restored to health by drinking Harrogate spring water. One example was a Mr William Tompson of Wetherby who was 'given over as a man past hope', who, after 14 days of treatment, was 'restored to be a perfect man, and so continueth'.

The Old Magnesia Well Pump Room was built in 1858 in Valley Gardens and was used as a place to serve mineral water. (Valley Gardens is the site of numerous springs, the waters of which contain iron or sulphur.) The Pump Room is now an interpretive centre, where you can learn more about Harrogate's watery history.

ADDRESS Valley Gardens, Harrogate, North Yorkshire, HG2 0DN, +44 (0)1423 525149, www.visitnorthyorkshire.com **TIP** Go for a swim or enjoy a spa treatment at the Turkish Baths Harrogate (www.turkishbathsharrogate.co.uk).

15 Calvary

Go on a pilgrimage

Peter Middleton was a prominent Victorian landowner who lived in Myddelton Lodge, less than a mile north of Ilkley. The Middletons were devout Catholics and Peter was no exception. To show his devotion he had a unique religious site built on his land: the Ilkley Calvary or the Stations of the Cross. Peter, according to an article in the *Northern Weekly Gazette* in 1899, 'erected this little oratory in which to take a daily walk', where he could 'meditate on holy things'. Happily, Calvary is now open to the public.

You are greeted at the entrance gate with a large metal plaque depicting a lamb supporting a cross, and the words '*Ex sequatur me et tollat crucem suam*', which is Latin for 'Let him (or her) follow me and take up his (or her) cross'. This is taken from the Vulgate Bible and is an instruction found in the gospels of Matthew and Luke. It instructs followers of Jesus that they should be prepared to accept the possibility of daily suffering, self-denial and the need to make personal sacrifices for their faith.

A short walk from the gate takes you to the first of 14 Stations of the Cross. Each numbered station represents a particular event on the last day of Christ's life as described in the Bible, starting with Christ being condemned to death, and ending with his body being laid in the tomb. Believers move in numerical order from station to station, meditating on the event depicted and reciting a specific prayer until all 14 stations have been visited. In older churches the stations are usually either realistic paintings or sculptures. Modern churches often take a more minimal or abstract approach. The stations in the Ilkley Calvary are sensibly carved from blocks of sandstone. At the end of the walkway is a grotto on top of which are three crosses that represent the crucifixion. If you're that way inclined, Good Friday, the day on which Christ was crucified, is an especially fitting day to make this mini pilgrimage.

ADDRESS Ilkley, LS29 0ED, West Yorkshire, dumps.udder.chops **TIP** Ilkley Moor Cow and Calf Rocks is an outcrop of millstone grit that offers a splendid view of Ilkley and across to the Yorkshire Dales.

16 Darwin Gardens

Highly evolved

Charles Darwin developed a deep interest in the natural world when he was young. However, when he enrolled at the University of Edinburgh in 1825 it was to study medicine not nature. Unfortunately, Darwin soon discovered that he was squeamish. Seeing a child undergo surgery without the benefit of anaesthesia was enough to put him off medicine for life. Ironically, given his later agnosticism, Darwin then enrolled at Cambridge to study theology.

In 1831, Darwin was offered a role on the HMS *Beagle*, a Royal Navy ship whose crew were tasked with undertaking a five-year, round-the-world voyage of scientific research. Darwin was not, however, hired as the ship's naturalist, but as a gentleman companion to Robert Fitzroy, captain of the *Beagle*.

The time Darwin spent on the *Beagle* was the making of him. The observations he made on the voyage led to the theory of evolution through natural selection that Darwin later described in *On the Origin of Species*, published in 1859. Unfortunately, however, the voyage had a less welcome effect on Darwin. It is thought that he contracted Chagas disease on his travels. This is an acute and potentially debilitating illness caused by the parasite *Trypanosoma cruzi*. This notion hasn't been accepted by everyone, however. It has also been argued that Darwin suffered from simple lactose intolerance. Whatever the cause, for the rest of his life he suffered from a variety of symptoms including vertigo, vomiting, headaches and insomnia.

Darwin tried every treatment available. In the autumn of 1859, he came to Ilkley to take the baths at the White Wells Spa. Darwin's two-month stay in Ilkley obviously worked, as he wrote in his diary that 'The Water Cure has done me much good'. In 2000, to celebrate the naturalist's visit to the town, the splendid Darwin Gardens were opened by novelist Jilly Cooper. There you can investigate the natural world just like an intrepid Victorian explorer.

ADDRESS Wells Road, Ilkley, LS29 9TF, West Yorkshire, www.darwingardens.org.uk
TIP Follow in the footsteps of Darwin and dip a toe in the (unheated) plunge pool at the 18th-century White Wells Spa on Ilkley Moor.

17 The Toy Museum

Childhood memories

In 1997, a collection of toys from the Ribchester Museum of Childhood was put up for auction at Hartley's in Ilkley. The night before the auction, Alex Samuel said to John, her husband, that 'Ilkley would be a good place to have a toy museum'. And so the pair decided to buy some toys. In 2001, after adding more playthings to the collection, the couple opened their dream museum.

The museum is a delightful cornucopia of toys past and present, and includes dolls and teddy bears, as well as games and educational playthings. By far the oldest toy in the collection is a delicate terracotta Corinthian dancing doll, made in the early fourth century B.C. Fully articulated, the female figure wears a sphendone, an ornamental headband, which is nestled in her curly hair. She is probably holding a pair of castanets in her left hand, a percussive instrument still used by dancers across the Mediterranean region today.

The most tragic exhibit has to be Thomas, the sad bear. Thomas was probably made in 1930 and belonged to a two-year-old boy named Jonathan. Sadly, Jonathan drowned on a family holiday in Norfolk. Touchingly, when Jonathan was found he was still clutching Thomas. It is all too easy to anthropomorphise, but Thomas really *does* seem to have a mournful expression.

It was long thought that boys would never want to play with dolls. This assumption was disproved by the success of Action Man, launched in the UK by Palitoy in 1966. The thoroughly rugged hero could be dressed in any number of uniforms, and equipped with a range of handy tools and fearsome weapons. The Toy Museum naturally has a number of Action Men on display, as well as a wide variety of toy soldiers large and small from across the centuries.

Adult visitors are often heard saying 'I used to have one of those'. It seems that the Toy Museum is truly a place to revert to a state of childhood wonder. And when has that ever been a bad thing?

ADDRESS 2 Whitton Croft Road, Ilkley, West Yorkshire, LS29 9HR, +44 (0)7808 762982, www.ilkleytoymuseum.co.uk TIP Relax and take afternoon tea in the wonderfully warm and welcoming Little Teahouse just five minutes' walk from the Toy Museum.

18 Twisleton Scar

Crazy paving

One thing you can't do in the Yorkshire Dales is visit the seaside. If you do feel the need to spend a day at the coast then you'll need to leave God's own country for the delights of (whisper it) Lancashire. Or – and this may be preferable if Morecambe Bay doesn't appeal – travel back in time some 330 million years to the Carboniferous era. At this point in prehistory, what would eventually become the Dales was a shallow tropical sea teeming with such creatures as shellfish, crinoids and coral reefs.

When these animals died, their hard parts – their shells and skeletons – drifted to the sea floor. Over time this created layers of calcium carbonate that gradually formed thick beds of limestone. This wasn't the end of the story, however. Over the millennia, the limestone beds slowly moved north and were uplifted to their present location. They were then scoured by glaciers during a long sequence of ice ages. These etched cracks and fissures into the limestone, eventually creating a geological formation known as limestone pavement. The escarpment of Twisleton Scar, overlooking Ingleton at the southern end of Kingsdale, is a very fine example of this distinctive type of landscape.

Geologists use a variety of words to describe the features of limestone pavements. A gryke (or grike) is the vertical fissure in the limestone. The web of grykes in the limestone leaves isolated blocks (the 'paving slabs' in the pavement) known as clints. You can also see solution cups, or hollows, in the pavement, as well as runnels, or channels created by rainwater. This creates a unique habitat that is home to plants such as baneberry and bloody crane's-bill, as well as various species of spleenwort. It is, however, a delicate landscape and one that could so easily be lost to quarrying and other human activities. Fortunately, since the Limestone Pavement Orders were passed in the late 1990s, they are protected environments.

ADDRESS Ingleton, LA6 3PH, North Yorkshire, perfected.slept.trailer **TIP** After walking up to Twisleton Scar, ease those aching joints by going for a refreshing swim in Ingleton's community-owned outdoor swimming pool (www.ingletonpool.co.uk).

19 Yordas Cave

Hidden depths

The now largely overlooked Yordas Cave was a popular show cave in the 18th and 19th centuries. One of the earliest descriptions of a visit was made in *A Tour to the Caves*, written by John Hutton and published in 1780. After a stop at a pub to 'procure a guide, candles, lanthorn, tinder-box & c., for the purpose of seeing Yordas Cave', Hutton made his way down Kingsdale to his destination.

The singular prospect of entering the gloomy depths of Yordas Cave obviously had an effect on Hutton, for he admitted that 'a thousand ideas were excited in my imagination on my entrance into this gloomy cavern, which had been for many years dormant'. Despite these thoughts, Hutton found his way inside where he discovered that 'the roof was so high, and the bottom and the sides so dark, that with all the light we could procure from our candles and torches we could not see the dimensions of this cavern'.

Illumination technology has improved considerably since Hutton's day; a modern LED torch will reveal details that would remain hidden by the feeble light of a candle. Even armed with a 21st-century torch, though, there is still a delicious thrill of anticipation on entering a mysterious and inky black subterranean space.

The Council for the Northern Caving Community state that no hazards have been reported for Yordas, but that doesn't mean that you should be complacent. As well as a bright torch, good boots are highly recommended. Rockfalls are uncommon but a caving helmet wouldn't go amiss. Once you're kitted up, make your way uphill on the path from Thornton Lane and then go through a gate to a wooded area and the surprisingly small entrance to Yordas.

The cave is a chamber 180 feet long and 49 feet wide. Cross the beck that runs down the length of the cavern. The most striking feature is found in the far corner. This is the Chapter House, a small chamber that contains a 25-foot-high waterfall.

ADDRESS Ingleton, LA6 3PH, North Yorkshire, along.protected.flanks TIP Follow the path along the Turbary Road to see Jingling Pot and Rowten Pot, two deep vertical shafts that lead down into the West Kingsdale Cave System.

20 Market Cross

Gather round for a bargain

Market towns such as Kirkby Lonsdale often feature a structure known as a market cross. These mark the spot where a market could be held, that right granted by the reigning monarch, a local baron or bishop. Kirkby Lonsdale goes one better than other towns by boasting *two* market crosses. The first – and older – can be found tucked away in Swinemarket, a cobbled square just off Mill Brow. This simple stone column is medieval and once stood at the junction of Main Street and Market Street until it was moved to its current and more obscure location in 1822.

The second cross is *far* more elaborate and harder to miss. This cross dominates Market Square at the centre of Kirkby Lonsdale, though rather unfortunately it's usually surrounded by cars making use of the neighbouring pay-and-display car park. The best time to experience the handsome market cross is on a Thursday, when cars are temporarily banished in favour of the weekly Charter Market. In 1227, John de Kirkby, a local parson, was granted the right to hold a weekly market as well as an annual fair in September. The town of Kirkby Lonsdale has exercised those rights ever since.

This newer market cross was erected in 1905. It was designed by a Mr J. F. Curwen of Kendal in the Tudor Gothic style popular at the time, and is octagonal in shape. The builders used a wonderfully honey-coloured sandstone, which has been elaborately detailed in places. These details include castellations, stone pillars and a roof-mounted cross. Running around the outer walls of the cross is a dedication, written in Gothic script, declaring that 'This Market Cross was presented to the town by the Rev J.W. Davies D.D. Vicar of Kirkby-Lonsdale from 1889 to 1908. 1905'. On 3 March, 1905, the *Lancashire Standard* reported that the chairman of the town's district council 'accepted the gift on behalf of the inhabitants, and Dr. Davies was warmly thanked for his generosity'.

ADDRESS Market Square, Kirkby Lonsdale, Cumbria, LA6 2AN, www.kirkbylonsdale.co.uk **TIP** Be sure to take a stroll to the Devil's Bridge and see if you can spot the 'devil's handprint' at the apex of the bridge.

21 Salt Pie Lane

'Anyone fancy a pint?'

There was once a regular cattle market in Kirkby Lonsdale, and nearby Salt Pie Lane was known logically as Cattle Market Yard. Seeing a business opportunity, an entrepreneurial lady who lived on the lane started selling hot pies to the market traders. One ingredient the wily baker freely added was salt. As intended, this made the market traders thirsty so that they were then more likely to go for a pint at the nearby Green Dragon public house, now the Snooty Fox. By no coincidence whatsoever, the landlord of the Green Dragon happened to be a relative of the pie maker. Such was the fame of the pie maker that the lane was renamed in her honour.

Salt Pie Lane isn't the only curiously named place in Kirkby Lonsdale. Just 10 minutes' walk away are the Radical Steps, which lead steeply down to the river Lune. These are named after Dr Francis Pearson, who was known locally for his politically radical views. A touching tribute to a well-loved pillar of the community? Not in the slightest. The name is sarcastic, designed to mock the doctor for his pretensions. The steps were built in 1820 because Pearson wanted to divert a public footpath that happened to pass through his garden at Abbots Brow. He had to obtain a court order to do so, which wasn't a popular move in the town.

The first half of the name Kirkby Lonsdale reflects the Scandinavian influence on the area. *Býr* is Old Norse for town or settlement and was used extensively across English territory conquered by the Vikings. There are numerous examples in northern England, such as Langwathby, Melmerby and Lazonby. The 'Kirk' prefix denotes the presence of a church, so Kirkby means 'settlement with a church'. Lonsdale derives from the river Lune and *dæl*, which is the Old English word for valley. An enjoyable way to explore a short section of the valley is to follow the path from the bottom of the Radical Steps to the Devil's Bridge half a mile away.

ADDRESS Kirkby Lonsdale, Cumbria, LA6 2AH, www.kirkbylonsdale.co.uk TIP Pay a visit to St Mary's Church and experience the cunning self-closing churchyard gates, erected in 1823.

22 The Vault

Bank on high levels of interest

There's a real joy to be had in listening to a tale well told. This is particularly true if that tale helps you gain a deeper understanding of a person or a place. The Vault, an interactive experience in Kirkby Lonsdale's Visitor Information Centre, achieves this happy state of affairs very agreeably indeed.

The concept is wonderfully simple and straightforward. Go to one of the safety deposit boxes in the vault and remove the object within. Place the item on the table and watch and listen to an associated narrative unfold in front of you. There are 11 objects in total, each one of which tells a different story about a significant figure or event in the history of Kirkby Lonsdale. It's utterly enchanting and thoroughly absorbing.

There are countless stories that could be told about a town with as much history as Kirkby Lonsdale. Some of these are inevitably sad. Take the account relayed in the *Newcastle Courant* on 10 May, 1800, for instance. A severe storm resulted in a soldier being 'found in a state of insensibility upon the road, a few miles from Kirby Lonsdale'. He was taken to the nearest home but 'expired in a few minutes'. The soldier was not the only victim that day. A woman with a young infant was discovered by the roadside by two travellers. The mother and child were both exhausted with fatigue and cold. One of the travellers remained with the women while the other rode to the town with the child to seek help. Tragically despite 'every possible endeavour to restore it', the child died within a few hours.

A happier tale is the Celebration of Peace held on 29 May, 1856, following the end of the Crimean War. According to the *Lancaster Guardian*, the 'shops were closed, and the bells of the Parish Church pealed forth their merry chimes at intervals throughout the day'. Later, 'a substantial tea was provided by subscription', and, '500 to 600 persons sat down and refreshed themselves'.

ADDRESS 29 Main Street, Kirkby Lonsdale, Cumbria, LA6 2AH, +44 (0)1524 297177, www.kirkbylonsdale.co.uk TIP If you enjoy jigsaws then you need to pay a visit to The Book and Jigsaw Lounges in Kirkby Lonsdale (www.thebooklounge.shop).

23 The Loki Stone

Marvellous

There aren't many churches in Britain that can boast their own resident Norse god. In fact there's only one: Kirkby Stephen Parish Church. Walk through the main entrance and you immediately come face to face with a representation in stone of Loki, a shape-shifting god with a reputation for trickery and low cunning. He was also said by believers to be the cause of unwanted knots or tangles in rope and cords, as well as the inventor of the fishing net. It was foretold that Loki would, along with fellow travellers, go to war with the gods of Asgard, such as Odin and Thor, to bring about *Ragnarök*, an apocalyptic time of upheaval known in English as the 'Twilight of the Gods'.

Loki is now, along with Thor, very much a household name thanks to the various superhero movies and TV shows set in the Marvel Cinematic Universe. The devious god with numerous plans for universal domination is played with great charm by British actor Tom Hiddleston, who you can tell truly relishes the chance to play Loki every time he appears onscreen.

The Loki stone in Kirkby Stephen Parish Church dates from the ninth or possibly tenth century. Perhaps fittingly, given Loki's mischievous ways, it is not known how the stone found its way to Kirkby Stephen. It was rediscovered in 1847 during restoration work to the chancel and put on display then. The figure on the stone is horned and appears to be bound by a thick strap. This fits in with the legend of Loki, who was wrapped in his own entrails after bringing about the death of Baldr, a favoured son of Odin.

However, there are some who think that the figure is not Loki at all but Wayland the Smith, another figure from Norse legend. Others believe that he is just a generic bound devil, so more Christian than Nordic in origin. Perhaps, though, that's just what Loki wants you to think…

ADDRESS Kirkby Stephen Parish Church, Kirkby Stephen, Cumbria, CA17 4QX, www.ksparishchurch.com TIP See a range of Victorian carriages and wagons, as well as steam and diesel locomotives, at Kirkby Stephen East railway station (www.kirkbystepheneast.co.uk).

24 The Nine Standards

Count them carefully

Near the summit of Hartley Fell, 2,130 feet above sea level, is an incongruous line of tall drystone cairns. Similar in shape to pepper-pots, these cairns are something of a puzzle. No one now knows who built them, why they did so or even when. Occasionally there are more than nine cairns and sometimes there are fewer. Locals keep an eye on things, however, and take down or rebuild as many cairns as necessary to return the number to nine. They also take great care to repair the cairns whenever they are damaged, particularly after bad winter weather has taken its toll.

The Nine Standards are first mentioned in 1507 in a record from East Stainmore, reported in a Brough Court paper of 1617. This means that the Nine Standards are at least 500 years old, but are probably far older than this. They are named on a parchment map that was possibly drawn in the mid 1600s, and were shown on the first Ordnance Survey map of the area in 1862. In 2005, low-level aerial photos of Hartley Fell appeared to show a rectangular enclosure around the Nine Standards. This is now thought to be a cashel, a type of fortification, that dates back to the Iron Age.

On 24 February, 1849, a writer for the *Kendal Mercury and Northern Advertiser* described the Nine Standards as 'nine huge obelisks of stone' but admitted that 'whether erected as boundary marks, or for some other purpose we have no evidence to show'. The writer also noted that 'tradition, however, avers that they were set up in time of war, and clothed in military array, in order to make the enemy believe that they were the van of an advancing enemy'. We are just as clueless about the intended purpose of the Nine Standards today. The most likely explanation is that they are a boundary marker, or possibly a useful waypoint for travellers crossing the fells. One thing *is* certain, however. They are a *far* more attractive landmark than the nearby modern trig point.

ADDRESS Kirkby Stephen, CA17 4JF, reckon.recliner.chop **TIP** Frank's Bridge over the river Eden is a handsome 17th-century double-arched packhorse bridge and Grade II-Scheduled Monument.

25 Pendragon Castle

Pull the Uther one

This could come as a shock so you may want to sit down. Arthur – king of the Britons, knight of the Round Table, husband to Guinevere, friend of Merlin, and dedicated seeker of the Holy Grail – never actually existed. There may well have been a Celtic chieftain or warlord called Arthur who lived in that murky historical period known as the Dark Ages. But, he definitely *wasn't* the dashing if flawed hero described in countless books, or shown in movies and – more recently – in video games.

If Arthur is fictional then so too is Uther Pendragon, Arthur's father. Uther is less celebrated than Arthur despite being (allegedly) as great a warrior as his son and, after many battles and adventures, also being crowned king of the Britons. His reputation is tarnished by his lust for and eventual seduction of Ygraine, wife of Gorlois, Duke of Cornwall and loyal ally of Uther. Happily, the result of this union was Arthur. Less happily, Gorlois was killed in battle by the wicked king's army during the siege of Dimilioc.

One curious aspect of Arthurian legend is the number of places in Britain in which Arthur (supposedly) lived. His stronghold was either in South Wales or Cornwall depending on who you believe. And he is said to lie asleep under a hill in Northumberland until his services are required once more. Uther, however, spent his final years living in a castle he (reputedly) had built in the Mallerstang valley, close to the river Eden. It was in this stronghold that he was murdered by Saxons after they sneakily poisoned his well.

Needless to say, the eponymous Pendragon Castle in Mallerstang has nothing to do with Arthur's dad. The now-ruined castle was built by the Normans in the 12th century. One (real) owner was Hugh de Morville, one of four knights who, in 1170, killed Thomas Becket, Archbishop of Canterbury. It was a brutal act of political vengeance that would have horrified Arthur (probably).

ADDRESS Kirkby Stephen, Cumbria, CA17 4JT, www.yorkshiredales.org.uk, amount. guards motorist TIP Kirkby Stephen's striking Temperance Hall was built in 1856 for those locals who had taken the pledge and given up drinking.

26 Arncliffe

Soap Sugdens

The 16 October, 1972, was something of a red-letter day for rural soap opera fans who happened to live in Yorkshire *and* who weren't at work or school. It was on this day that the very first episode of the long-running drama series *Emmerdale Farm* was broadcast. At 1.30 in the afternoon. And not to every region in the ITV network. Fortunately, the new Yorkshire Television production quickly proved popular with viewers. By 1977, the soap was regularly watched by 10 million people across the country and had been moved in the schedules to a more favourable evening slot. And the name of the soap? Amerdale was an old name for Littondale. Change the spelling a bit and you have Emmerdale.

Fittingly, every episode of the soap has been filmed in Yorkshire; the outdoor scenes in the Yorkshire Dales and the interiors at Yorkshire Television's (now ITV's) studios in Leeds. Between 1972 and 1975, the village of Arncliffe in Littondale was the stand-in for the fictional Beckindale. The local pub, The Falcon Inn, became The Woolpack. And Arncliffe's church and vicarage, forge and village shop were also frequently seen onscreen. In 1976, however, the production team decided that the frequent travelling backwards and forwards to Arncliffe was expensive and inconvenient. And so shooting moved to Esholt, north of Bradford, ending Arncliffe's all-too-brief moment in the sun.

Visit Arncliffe today and you can see why it was originally chosen by YTV to represent Beckindale. The village is small but perfectly formed, utterly charming and unspoilt. Traditional stone houses (of which 20 are listed) line a large grassy village square, which still features a stone water pump. And the Falcon Inn serves beer, which you can opt to have served from a jug the old-fashioned way. Visit Arncliffe and you'll have a good time, without any drama or even a commercial break halfway through.

ADDRESS Arncliffe, Skipton, North Yorkshire, BD23 5QD, www.yorkshiredales.co.uk
TIP Arncliffe, particularly the village's bridge over the river Skirfare, is thought to have inspired Charles Kingsley to write *The Water-Babies*, published in 1863.

27 The Cathedral of the Dales

Inspirational

St Michael the Archangel is the impressively large parish church of Malhamdale. The church is also (justifiably) known locally as the Cathedral of the Dales. St Michael's has had its fair share of notable visitors over the years, one of whom was Charles Kingsley. The author visited the church in 1858 while staying at Tarn House in Malham. It's thought that a number of locations in the Dales inspired places and events in Kingsley's children's novel *The Water-Babies*, published in 1863. The bells of St Michael must have affected Kingsley for they are referred to in a song heard by Tom on one of his adventures: 'Under the crag where the ouzel sings/And the ivied wall where the church-bell rings'.

Another possible visitor was Oliver Cromwell. His name was signed into a (since stolen) parish register, and he may have been a witness to a wedding or two there. The first couple were John Ellin and Anne Tayler. They were married on '25th July in the presence of John Lawson of Malham & John Shackleton of the same & others before me, Olyver Cromwell R'. However, there is some doubt as to the authenticity of the signature. Cromwell is known to have been in London on 28 July. Three days' difference may not seem much, but travelling between Malham and the capital in that time would have been near impossible in the 1650s.

One curious monument in the churchyard is the 'Watery Grave', which straddles a small stream. This is the last resting place of Helen Harrison and her husband, Colonel John Harrison, a wealthy businessman from Bradford. Helen originally planned to be buried on one side of the stream and her husband on the other. However, rocky ground made the request impossible and so the two were conventionally buried side by side. Why Helen wanted to spend eternity separated from her spouse is a detail now sadly lost to history.

ADDRESS St Michael the Archangel Church, Kirkby Malham, North Yorkshire, BD23 4BS, www.kirkbymalhamchurch.org TIP See the exquisite metalwork of blacksmith Annabelle Bradley at Malhamdale Smithy (www.malhamsmithyonline.co.uk).

28 Gordale Scar

Natural wonder

What does the word 'romantic' mean to you? Unbidden flowers and chocolates, possibly? Or perhaps being whisked away to spend a long weekend in a European city of culture, such as Leeds? These are all perfectly valid definitions. However, like many words in the English language, romantic has a number of meanings. One of these relates to a loose group of artists active at the tail end of the 18th century and a good way into the next.

The Romantic movement resulted in an entirely new way of looking at the world. Until then, wild landscapes were generally seen as dangerous and best avoided if at all possible. Painters, such as John Martin and J. M. W. Turner, began to depict nature in a more sympathetic and imaginative way. Their work was designed to invoke a strong emotional response in the viewer, emotions such as awe and wonder. These artists also felt that it was important to immerse themselves in impressive landscapes, and so actively sought out places that would inspire them.

Gordale Scar was one of those places. The scar is a deep ravine with cliffs over 330 feet high, created when the local limestone was eroded by glacial meltwater as a series of ice ages over the past 100,000 years or so came to a soggy end. Gordale Beck, which flows through the gorge, is an insignificant trickle compared with the mighty torrents that helped form the gorge.

One artist inspired by Gordale Scar was James Ward, who – in 1815 – first exhibited *Gordale Scar (A View of Gordale, in the Manor of East Malham in Craven, Yorkshire, the Property of Lord Ribblesdale)*. This magnificent painting is darkly menacing, and depicts towering cliffs silhouetted by turbulent stormy light in the sky above. If ever a painting could be described as Romantic (with that all-important capital R) it is this particular piece. It is possibly not a place your nearest and dearest would appreciate, however.

ADDRESS Malham, North Yorkshire, BD23 4DL, www.yorkshiredales.co.uk, width.reclined.presenter **TIP** Janet's Foss is a charming small waterfall on Gordale Beck, a short distance from Gordale Lane in a wooded glade.

29 Malham Cove

Where's the water?

Charles Lyell was a Victorian geologist whose multi-volume work *Principles of Geology* fundamentally changed how we view our planet. Until then, it was generally thought that the Earth had been shaped purely by huge cataclysmic events. Lyell proposed that geological changes were (generally) more gradual and were caused by observable processes, such as the slow but remorseless way water and wind erode rocky features. Lyell's idea is known as uniformitarianism and is the foundation of modern geological thinking.

Our short lives make it difficult to appreciate how gradually landscapes change. Take Malham Cove, for instance. It may look solid and permanent but it's very much a work in progress. The cove is formed from limestone deposited during the Carboniferous some 360–330 million years ago. This was a time when the Dales were at a more tropical latitude and were covered by a warm sea.

The 260-foot high cliff was created by the scouring action of ice as it formed and then melted during the various ice ages of the past 60,000 years. At one point, the melting ice created a huge waterfall that would have cascaded spectacularly down the face. The water now sinks underground into a complex cave system roughly a mile north of the cove. Rain continues to erode the limestone; millennia of wet weather created the distinctive limestone pavement on the cliff top and will continue to shape it for millennia to come.

Although geological forces grind slowly, humanity has occasionally contemplated changing the area more rapidly. A report in the *Yorkshire Post* on 11 October, 1938 noted that Malham Cove 'has survived several attempts to deprive it of its natural beauty'. This included bungalow builders who had 'envious eyes on the spot for a long time' as well as enthusiastic if misguided scientists 'who wanted to blast a way into the cave behind the cove'. Thankfully, neither scheme came to fruition.

ADDRESS Malham, North Yorkshire, BD23 4DJ, www.yorkshiredales.co.uk **TIP** After your walk, refresh yourself with a cup of tea and a slice of cake at The Old Barn Tearoom in Malham (www.oldbarnmalham.co.uk).

30 Himalayan Garden and Sculpture Park

Shangri-La

In 1996, the Hutts in Grewelthorpe – what would eventually become the Himalayan Garden and Sculpture Park – was a less-than-inspiring mix of coppiced hazel woodland and dense sitka spruce plantation, infested by tangles of Japanese knotweed. However, it was in this year that Peter and Caroline Roberts acquired the property, and they had a plan.

The driveway into the Hutts was lined with rhododendron. This prompted Peter to visit established rhododendron gardens across the country, such as Ray Wood at Castle Howard, and Bodnant. With the help of expert Alan Clark, the Hutts was gradually populated with different varieties of rhododendron, as well as azaleas, magnolias and other unusual plants. Peter even travelled to the Himalayas to acquire new and novel specimens to add to the rapidly developing garden. The 45-acre site was soon transformed into a wonderfully exotic and verdant space. Today there are nearly 20,000 different plants growing in the garden, of which some 1,400 are various types of rhododendron. There are also 90 contemporary sculptures, placed sympathetically to enhance the garden.

The public were first given a peek at Peter and Caroline's creation on 31 May, 1998, when the gardens were opened in aid of the North Yorkshire St John Ambulance. Proceeds from the admissions, homemade teas and plant sales were all donated to the charity, a big-hearted gesture repeated annually for years afterwards.

The Himalayan Garden and Sculpture Park is now in the care of the Hutts Foundation, set up by Peter and Caroline. This charitable trust is tasked with looking after the garden and sharing it with the public. The foundation also has an educational remit, as well as the all-important job of promoting the conservation of rare and endangered plant species here in Britain and across the world.

ADDRESS The Hutts, Hutts Lane, Grewelthorpe, Ripon, North Yorkshire, HG4 3DA, +44 (0)1765 658009, www.himalayangarden.com, battling.homecare.spits TIP Just two miles west as the crow flies, the Druid's Temple is a 19th-century folly built to resemble a prehistoric stone circle.

31 Thornborough Henges

'Like a wheel within a wheel'

Masham is a modern market town but you don't have to look far to find something created in its dim and distant past. At St Mary's Church, for instance, you can view the remains of a ninth-century cross in the churchyard. However, take a short drive east, and you can visit a site that is truly ancient: Thornborough Henges.

A henge is a circular or oval enclosure consisting of a ditch and a raised bank of earth, built during the Neolithic between 3000 and 2000 B.C. Britain's best-known henge is Stonehenge, which has a dramatic stone circle at its centre. There are three henges at Thornborough, none with a central stone circle, though the complex is often referred to as the 'Stonehenge of the North'. The three henges are all roughly 790 feet in diameter and are arrayed in a slightly crooked straight line 3,600 feet from one end to the other. Intriguingly, the layout resembles the position of the three stars that form the 'belt' in the constellation of Orion.

The most northerly henge is currently covered in a copse of trees. Ironically, this is the best preserved of the three henges, though the other two are still spectacular in their scale. There is no evidence that definitively proves why the henges were built. However, it's likely that they had a role in religious ceremonies and rituals.

This unique site was in danger of being seriously damaged by farm livestock as well as being undermined by rabbits. In 2009, the complex was ignominiously put on the Heritage at Risk register, an annual report published by Historic England. Fortunately, the owners of the land – Tarmac and Lightwater Holdings – gifted the site to the nation in 2023. They are now managed by English Heritage and are freely accessible to everyone. As the then-chief executive of Historic England, Duncan Wilson, said at the time of the donation, 'they are a link to our ancient ancestors, through thousands of years, inspiring a sense of wonder and mystery'.

ADDRESS New Lane, West Tanfield, Ripon, North Yorkshire, DL8 2RD, www.english-heritage.org.uk, grins.disclose.charts TIP At first glance you'd think that Mowbray Castle in the grounds of Hackfall Wood is a ruined medieval castle. It's actually a wonderfully detailed folly built for William Aislabie in the mid-17th century (www.hackfall.org.uk).

32 The Coldstones Cut

Epic art

There have been limestone quarries on the slopes of Greenhow Hill for almost 200 years. In February, 1893, an edition of the *Pateley Bridge and Nidderdale Herald* printed an advert placed by H. Newbould and Bros. The company had recently opened a quarry and were 'now prepared to receive orders' for their product. Coldstones Quarry is the last quarry still operating in the area and its scale is truly staggering.

The quarry was excavated at the very summit of Greenhow Hill roughly 1,400 feet above sea level, and covers an area of approximately 75 acres. The benefit of the quarry being at the top of a hill is that it is essentially out of sight; you can only see it by making the effort of walking or driving up to the site. The limestone is extracted from six separate terraces or 'benches', each 50 feet or so in height, with the quarry itself roughly 985 feet deep.

Coldstones Quarry is award winning. The owners were presented with a Special Award by the judges of the 1998 Harrogate Council's Design Awards. The judges particularly appreciated the considerate 'manner in which the quarry was run and the way staff involved themselves with the local community at Greenhow, worked with the Nidderdale schools and looked after flora and fauna on the site'. The company was also mindful of the fact that the quarry is within the Nidderdale Area of Outstanding Beauty and 'the impact modern quarrying can have in such an environment'.

The best place to appreciate the grandeur of the quarry is from Coldstones Cut. This is a wonderfully rugged and monumental piece of public art created by sculptor Andrew Sabin. Coldstones Cut opened in 2010 and directly overlooks the quarry. The main viewing platform offers a panoramic view of the quarry, and features a long information panel that helpfully points out the distance to towns in Yorkshire and elsewhere in the world.

ADDRESS Bewerley, North Yorkshire, HG3 5JQ, www.thecoldstonescut.org, uncouth.disarmed.covertly **TIP** A short trail from the car park takes you round Toft Gate Lime Kiln, a fascinating remnant of Nidderdale Victorian industry.

33 Heather Moorland

Purple patch

The Yorkshire Dales are undeniably beautiful but arguably they are at their best in late summer, between July and September. This is when the heather on upland moors is in bloom.

There are three types of heather commonly found in the Dales. The most abundant is ling heather (*Calluna vulgaris*) and it is this variety that dominates the moorlands. Ling heather is a woody shrub with small purple-pink flowers that provides food and shelter for a variety of creatures. The largest of these animals is the red grouse (*Lagopus lagopus scotica*), a characterful game bird with a call that can sound eerily like the chuckle of someone laughing at their own joke. Grouse eat heather shoots and it is for this reason that heather is often deliberately burned, a technique known as muirburn. This clears away the older woody stems of heather and encourages new shoots to come through.

Traditionally, ling heather was put to a number of uses. The Latin name *Calluna* is derived from the ancient Greek word for brush, and clumps of heather – when tied together – can be used as a very effective brush, known as a besom. Heather has also been used as thatch and as (surprisingly comfortable) bedding for both people and livestock. It can also be used as a dye and to tan leather. Bees like heather, and heather honey, which has a distinctive strong taste and is richly aromatic, is prized by connoisseurs.

The other, less widespread varieties (relatively speaking), are bell heather (*Erica cinerea*) and cross-leaved heath (*Erica tetralix*). As the name suggests, bell heather has large bell-shaped flowers that are more reddish-purple than those found on ling heather. The flowers of cross-leaved heath are similar to those of bell, though they are a paler pink. All three heather varieties thrive in acidic soils poor in nutrients, such as peatlands. So, if you want a wonderfully sensory experience this summer make a bee-line for the moors.

ADDRESS At various upland locations in the Yorkshire Dales National Park and Nidderdale National Landscape TIP Go on a trek accompanied by a llama (or alpaca) by booking an experience with Nidderdale Llamas (www.nidderdalellamas.org).

34 Jenny Twigg and her Daughter Tib

Murder most foul

There was once a woman called Jenny Twigg who, with her only daughter Tib, ran an inn on the slopes of Dead Man's Hill near Arkleside in Coverdale. The inn was far from the nearest village and so the only customers were drovers. These were men who took herds of cattle to market, on foot and often over great distances. One day, three drovers arrived at the inn looking for food and a bed for the night. The three were on their way home from market and coins jingled noisily in their pockets. Pitiless greed took hold of Jenny and Tib and they soon devised a cruel and brutal plan.

Once the men were asleep, the two women crept quietly from room to room. Callously wielding an axe, Jenny chopped off each man's head in turn as Tib relieved the victim of his money. The wicked pair then buried the now decapitated corpses on the moorland nearby. This heinous and bloody crime did not go unpunished, however. The mother and daughter were caught, tried and swiftly hanged for the murders.

It's a truly gruesome tale. And in 1728, the headless bodies of three Scottish pedlars were found on Dead Man's Hill. However, there's no evidence whatsoever that anyone named Jenny Twigg or Tib were involved. Not a single court record. Nothing. And yet the story is still widely circulated and referenced.

What does definitely exist are two tall columns of weatherbeaten millstone grit, marked on Ordnance Survey maps as Jenny Twigg and her Daughter Tib. These are not found in Coverdale, however, but on Sype Land in Nidderdale. These two columns are wonderfully described in *Nidderdale* by William Grainge (published in 1863) as having 'the appearance of giantesses in broad bonnets'. Perhaps this was how the felonious females were punished: turned to stone for their truly gruesome crime.

ADDRESS Sype Land near Lofthouse, North Yorkshire, handy.suits.paving TIP How Stean Gorge is a wonderfully atmospheric limestone gorge in Nidderdale National Landscape area (www.nidderdale-nl.org.uk).

35 The Oldest Sweetshop in the World

'Hello Sweetie!'

Pateley Bridge is a friendly market town nestled at the heart of Nidderdale. There are many wonderful local businesses on the high street but only one that features in the *Guinness World Records.* That business is the (accurately) named Oldest Sweetshop in the World. The shop has been selling its sweet treats continuously since 1827, and was recognised for this singular achievement in 2014.

The sweetshop has been family run since its inception. Just not necessarily the same family. Business entrepreneur Ben Howie bought the sweetshop in 2021 at the age of 23. For him it was a dream come true as he had regularly spent his pocket money there as a child. In an interview with the BBC that year, Ben stated that 'the history and heritage inside this shop is so interesting, everything from the floorboards upwards has history to it'. Despite the challenges of owning and running such an iconic venue, Ben was excited to 'continue the history of sweets and sweet making' in Pateley Bridge. And, in a nod to both the past and to the future, Ben felt that he was merely a 'custodian, rather than owner of the historic business'.

You can buy thoroughly modern sweets in the Oldest Sweetshop. Some things don't change, however. The best-selling sweets two centuries ago are still the most popular today. Hard-boiled treats such as rhubarb and custard, pear drops and humbugs are as tempting to our 21st-century palates as they were to our Victorian forebears. And these sweets are still made the old-fashioned way: the sugary mixture boiled in traditional copper pans.

Visiting the sweetshop is a heady experience. The shelves groan with rows of glass jars filled with an overwhelming choice of confectionery. The biggest problem you'll have is deciding what to buy. There's no need to worry though – you won't be hurried at all. You're encouraged to make a decision in your own sweet time.

ADDRESS 39 High Street, Pateley Bridge, North Yorkshire, HG3 5JZ, +44 (0)1423 712371, www.oldestsweetshop.co.uk **TIP** If you need to work off your sugar rush then take a stroll around Pateley Bridge's handsome recreation ground next to the river Nidd.

36 Stump Cross Caverns

The long game

Patience is a virtue. However, even the most worthy of us would get a wee bit restless if asked to watch a stalactite form. Stalactites are columns of rock that grow downwards from the roofs of limestone caves, forming in places where water regularly drips. As the droplets fall they leave tiny particles of calcite behind. Over time these particles build up (or rather down) to create the stalactite. These structures form *extremely* slowly: it takes roughly 1,000 years for a stalactite to grow four inches. Stalagmites sprout up from cave floors, usually in a wide and flat shape. Occasionally the two meet to form a column of rock many, *many* millennia in the making.

Stump Cross Caverns is a truly wonderful place to experience the magic of speleothems (the name for geological formations such as stalactites and stalagmites). The caverns were discovered in January 1860 by brothers Mark and William Newbould. The two were lead miners and were hoping to find a viable vein of lead ore below Craven Moor. It was in an exploratory shaft 52 feet deep that they broke into Stump Cross Caverns, a long natural cave system. The pair soon realised that they had struck (metaphorical) gold. Arranging a lease from the landowner, Thomas Yorke, William opened Moorcock Inn near the site. Visitors were charged one shilling to enter the cave, the entrance made easier by the creation of steps down into the cave in 1863.

Many of the speleothems in Stump Cross Caverns have imaginative and often witty names based on their shape: the Policeman's Truncheon, the Sleeping Cat, the Wedding Cake and the Hawk are just a few examples. You can also see other weird and wonderful formations such as rimstone pools (or gours) and helictites (a stalactite with a gravity-defying mind of its own). So fascinating are the caverns that you'll probably spend several hours there. Which is the time it would take a stalactite to grow 0.0000009055 inches…

ADDRESS Just off the B6265, Greenhow Hill, Pateley Bridge, North Yorkshire, HG3 5JL, +44 (0)1756 752780, www.stumpcrosscaverns.co.uk, fidelity.starring.landscape
TIP Although it's out-of-bounds to civilians, you won't be able to miss nearby RAF Menwith Hill – a 245-hectare electronic monitoring station.

37 Whittaker's Distillery

Bottoms up!

The first beer was brewed – probably by accident – roughly 10,000 years ago. Wine came along some four millennia later. Compared with these, gin is a (relative) newcomer on the scene. The invention of gin was originally credited to Dutch physician Franciscus Sylvius, who was said to have concocted the drink in the mid 17th century. However, the likeliest inventors were monks, who probably first distilled gin in the Netherlands in the 13th century.

Gin is a spirit distilled from barley (or another grain) and primarily flavoured with juniper berries. The name derives from genever, an older English word that has its roots in *juniperus*, the Latin for juniper. Gin became very popular in England during the reign of William and Mary when the government curiously allowed gin to be produced unlicensed. Unfortunately, this led to what would now be termed a health crisis, and known to history as the 'Gin Craze'. Gin was cheap and strong and drunk regularly by the poor as a way to temporarily escape from their troubles. The chaotic scene depicted in William Hogarth's print *Gin Lane* is the artist's warning on the perils of drinking gin excessively.

Gin's reputation was rescued by much-needed legislation in the late 18th century, and by the development of a more refined and delicate spirit (known as 'London Dry') in the 1830s. Gin is now a popular drink once more, and is produced (responsibly!) by distilleries across the country. One such distillery is the family-owned firm of Whittaker's in Nidderdale. Their artisanal Original Gin (one of a number of gins produced by the distillery) is also flavoured with botanicals such as bilberries and bog myrtle, which roots the drink in its moorland home. So good is this gin that it won Gold in the World Gin Awards in 2021. Whittaker's also produces a range of whiskies. Their first single malt was launched in August 2024, an achievement we can all raise a glass to.

ADDRESS Harewell House Farm, Dacre Banks, North Yorkshire, HG3 4HQ, +44 (0)1423 781842, www.whittakersdistillery.com, chat.magnum.undivided TIP Enjoy a day of traditional agricultural competition, as well as crafts and cricket matches, at the Nidderdale Show, held annually every September (www.nidderdaleshow.co.uk).

38 Yorke's Folly

Two stoops

A folly (or eye-catcher) is a building or structure constructed purely for amusement or to delight the eye, and that has no useful purpose. In the 18th and 19th centuries, the British upper classes went ever-so-slightly potty about follies, scattering them across their often vast estates with remarkable abandon. Very occasionally, however, there was method in the madness.

The stone structure that came to be known as Yorke's Folly was built on the slopes of Guisecliff for John Yorke, who inherited the Bewerley estate from his father in 1768. According to an article in the *Gazette and Times*, published on 17 September, 1898, Yorke had it built 'at a time of great distress, so that he might be able to provide work for the dalesmen, and save them from starvation'. The lucky labourers working on the folly were paid a shilling a day and given a loaf of bread for their troubles.

The folly was designed to resemble the ruins of an abbey, possibly modelled on Fountains Abbey just seven miles east of Bewerley. For most of the 19th century, Yorke's Folly was also known as the 'Three Stoops' after the three vertical columns that Yorke had built. The third, and ironically most substantial, 'stoop' was blown over during a particularly violent storm on 17 November, 1893.

Yorke died in 1813. A notice in *Drakard's Paper* stated that he was a 'gentleman long distinguished for his elegant taste in works of genius, and for the exercise of every Christian virtue, but more especially those of charity and benevolence'. Even more effusive was a description in *Nidderdale*, written by William Grange and published in 1863. Yorke, thanks to his 'highly cultivated mind, well stored with ancient and modern learning', was 'open to every liberal and humane idea'. When he died 'the poor lost in him a most bountiful benefactor'. This suggests that Yorke was a good man who managed to avoid the other follies that often accompany wealth.

ADDRESS Nought Moor, Nought Bank Road, North Yorkshire, www.nidderdale-nl.org.uk, dried.fortunes.yarn TIP Enjoy a hearty breakfast or lunch, including the soup of the day, at the Wildings Riverside Café.

39 Jubilee Clock

Now you're tocking

Princess Alexandrina Victoria of Kent wasn't born to be queen of Great Britain. The job was thrust upon her when her uncle, William IV, died in 1837 without children. Ironically, the reign of Victoria (as she styled herself once queen) would be one of the longest in British history, her record beaten only by Elizabeth II.

Victoria's Golden Jubilee in 1887 was heartily celebrated by a grateful nation. This commemoration took many forms. The good people of Otley erected a handsome clock tower, which is an iconic and still useful landmark in the town today.

The clock mechanism was built by Wm. Potts and Sons, who were based in Leeds. They were responsible for many other municipal timepieces in the area, including the Menston Asylum clock. The tower was built from stone and incorporates a handy drinking trough and access door. Fittingly, the entire structure is topped with an ornamental ironwork crown. Before the clock tower was completed, the writer of the 'Whispers' column ('A voice and nothing more') in the *Wharfedale and Airedale Observer* proudly stated that it 'will stand for ages to come as a memorial to Otley loyalty'. More breathlessly, the author hoped that the four clock faces would tell 'an honest tale as to the time of day, and in the darkest hours, its various countenances will be irradiated by the light of truth'.

Happily, 'Whispers' was there when the clock tower was formally opened at 4pm on 23 June, 1888. The honour of opening the clock was given to a 'Master Harold Duncan, aged five years, son of Mr T. A. Duncan of Westbourne Lodge', and 'the tiny official was lifted up in the arms of the policemen that all might see his bright, winsome, innocent face'. When young Harold set the heavy clock pendulum going, he said in a tiny voice 'three cheese for the Queen'. This left one witness wondering if 'Camembert, Roquefort or Gorgonzola would be offered'.

ADDRESS Kirkgate, Otley, West Yorkshire, LS21 3AQ, www.visitotley.co.uk, green.research.morphing **TIP** Shop for fresh produce and local crafts at the Otley Market, held in the Market Place every week on a Tuesday, Friday and Saturday.

40 Thomas Chippendale Statue

Street furniture

Otley was the birthplace of Thomas Chippendale, an 18th-century woodworker and furniture maker. Chippendale's furniture is very highly sought after nearly three centuries on. A piece known as the Harrington Commode (a type of washstand) was sold in 2010 by Christie's for an eye-watering £3,793,250, for example.

Chippendale was born in 1718, the only child of John and Mary Chippendale. Woodworking was in Chippendale's blood from the very start. John was a joiner and it's thought that young Thomas first learnt the basics of his trade from him. In the early 1750s, Chippendale opened a workshop in St Martin's Lane in London. In 1754 he published the first edition of *The Gentleman and Cabinet Maker's Director*, described on the front page as 'Being a large collection of the most elegant and useful designs of household furniture in the most fashionable taste'. The *Director* was *very* successful in promoting Chippendale's work and his patrons eventually included aristocrats, as well as self-made men such as actor David Garrick.

Otley is rightly proud of its association with Chippendale. On 26 January, 1965, the first meeting of the Chippendale Society was held, with Sir Malcolm Stoddart Scott, MP for Ripon, elected as the society's first president. Over the years the society has organised a number of events to promote the town's connection to Chippendale. The society's most striking achievement was the erection of a statue of Chippendale on the corner of Clapgate in 1987. The piece was created by sculptor Graham Ibbeson, who has also created statues of Eric Morecambe, Cary Grant, and Laurel and Hardy. Unlike these works, the representation of Chippendale is a more speculative likeness of the subject. Some people have even noted mischievously that the face of Chippendale bears more than a passing resemblance to Ibbeson's brother-in-law.

ADDRESS Clapgate, Otley, West Yorkshire, LS21 3HN, www.visitotley.co.uk, river.snippets.shrimp TIP The Navvies Memorial in Otley is an impressive stone structure that celebrates the men who lost their lives building the Bramhope Railway Tunnel.

41 River Bain

Record-breaking river

The mighty river Nile is some 4,100 miles in length, making it the longest waterway on Earth. There are numerous becks and rivers in the Yorkshire Dales though none are in any way comparable with the Nile. The Dales can't even claim the longest river in England either; that would be the 220-mile-long river Severn. They can, however, boast the longest river in Yorkshire: the 74-mile-long river Ure, which starts its journey to the sea (via the river Ouse) on Abbotside Common a few miles north of Garsdale Head. Happily, the Dales can claim a second watery record too. At a mere two and a half miles in length, the river Bain in Raydale is the shortest river in England. Possibly. The good folks of Sidmouth in Devon believe that their river – the Sid – has a better claim to the title.

The Bain flows out from Semer Water and snakes its way north to join the river Ure. It has been argued by Stefan Drew of the Sid Valley Biodiversity Group that this casts doubt on the Bain's status as a true river. In a thoughtful piece for the *Sidmouth Herald*, Drew asserted that the Bain 'has no real beginning, middle and end'. The Sid, on the other hand, although six miles in length and so nearly three times longer than the Bain, is 'a complete river. One that rises, flows and enters the sea at its end. Not a channel that joins to other bodies of water'. Drew rightly noted that 'there are those further north that will disagree with me'.

However, this is a competition between two English rivers. Just to muddy the waters (as it were), if you include the other three countries in the United Kingdom then the river Scavaig on the Isle of Skye would take the record. This decidedly wee watercourse is just a few hundred yards long. And then there's the river Morar in the west Highlands of Scotland. The Morar is roughly half a mile in length but is still crossed by three bridges *and* feeds a hydroelectric plant. Anyone not impressed by this must be in denial.

ADDRESS Northern end: Bainbridge, North Yorkshire, DL8 3EF, breathing.goggles.exchanges; southern end: near Low Blean Farm, Bainbridge, North Yorkshire, DL8 3DJ, phantom.ample.nudge TIP A (short!) section of Alfred Wainwright's 247-mile-long A Pennine Journey walk connects the southern end of the Bain to Bainbridge and its merging with the Ure.

42 Semer Water

Water way to go

According to the ancient Greek philosopher Plato, Atlantis was an imperial island state off the coast of Africa in the Atlantic Ocean. After failing to subjugate Athens, Atlantis was struck down by the gods and sank beneath the waves never to be seen again.

Plato was not writing dodgy history, however. He used Atlantis as an allegory for a civilisation that ultimately failed due to its many shortcomings. Despite the fact that Atlantis never existed, it has taken hold in the imagination of writers and artists ever since. What could be more thrilling than the thought that arrogance and hubris should have so terminal a punishment?

The Yorkshire Dales may (not really!) have their own Atlantis somewhere in the depths of Semer Water. And the story has striking similarities to that of Atlantis too. This is probably no coincidence. The tale unfolds something like this…

Once upon a time there was a city. The inhabitants were a proud and arrogant people not given to welcoming strangers. It was therefore unfortunate when a beggar arrived one day asking for shelter and food. The only folks willing to help were a poor couple who lived in a cottage outside the city on a nearby hill. They took the beggar in and offered him a bed for the night, which he gratefully accepted. The following morning, however, the beggar had vanished. Puzzled, the couple left their cottage to walk down to the city. Imagine their shock when they saw that it had disappeared below the surface of a new and very large lake. It is still said that when conditions are right it is possible even now to see the rooftops of the sunken buildings far below in the watery depths.

The truth is both more prosaic and interesting, geologically speaking. The second-largest natural lake in North Yorkshire, Semer Water was formed from glacier meltwater at the end of the last ice age, some 10,000 years before Plato was even born.

ADDRESS Low Blean Farm, Bainbridge, North Yorkshire, DL8 3DJ, +44 (0)1969 650436, www.lakesemerwater.co.uk, tribes.decisions.usages TIP Semer Water Nature Reserve is at the southern end of the lake. It's fairly easy to spot regular visitors such as curlew or lapwing but also look out for the rarer osprey that fish on the lake during the breeding season (www.ywt.org.uk).

43 Blea Moor Tunnel

Going underground

On 13 April, 1872, the *Knaresborough Post* ran a *very* tempting six-line advertisement in the 'Wanted' section of the classifieds, placed there on behalf of Midland Railway. The notice promised that 'GOOD MINERS may find Constant Employment at the Blea Moor Tunnel on above Wages 5s. to 5s. 6d. per day'. This promise proved to be accurate, for the 2,629-yard-long tunnel took hundreds of navvies more than four years to complete. It was a physically punishing experience. The tunnel was excavated using picks and shovels; the only machines employed were steam engines used to remove the spoil. And the weather on Blea Moor can be brutal, even in summer; in July 1870, several men working on cuttings on the moor were drowned by flash flooding following a rainstorm.

The hard work was worth it, for Blea Moor Tunnel is an engineering marvel. It is the longest tunnel on the Settle–Carlisle railway line. Trains gradually descend down an incline to a point some 500 feet below the moor. Seven vertical ventilation shafts were dug during construction of the tunnel, of which three are still in use; the squat brick chimneys of the shafts are useful landmarks on the footpath that crosses Blea Moor.

On 19 August, 1880, the Westinghouse (air) brake of a passenger train from Manchester failed and so the train was brought to a halt midway through the tunnel. Fifteen minutes later an express from London entered the tunnel. This train could not be stopped in time and crashed into the guard's van of the stationary train. Fortunately, no one was hurt though passengers on both trains were understandably shaken. Another accident occurred on 21 April, 1952, when a Thames–Clyde Express was derailed near the southern tunnel entrance by a loose brake rod hanging down from the leading engine. Thirty-two people were injured – 17 of whom were hospitalised – though happily there were no fatalities.

ADDRESS There's a good view of the tunnel entrance from a bridge over the railway on Blea Moor (chairing.willing.marshes); carry on along the path northwards to see the first of the air shafts (airbase.goodbyes.anguished) TIP You can get a good view of the Three Peaks (Ingleborough, Whernside and Pen-y-ghent) from the trig point on the Crag of Blea Moor (sifts.shun.stress).

44 Craven Lime Works

Travel back in time

On 12 October, 2002, a new and unusual visitor attraction opened in the Yorkshire Dales National Park. The Craven Lime Works is a small but significant heritage site that demonstrates how important industry once was to the Dales. The park authority took two years and spent £350,000 to conserve the lime works and provide visitors with information panels that tell the story of the works.

Craven Lime Works was established in 1873 to produce agricultural lime and mortar using the abundant supply of limestone from nearby Langcliffe Quarry. At the heart of the entire operation was the Hoffman continuous kiln. This is essentially a stone tunnel in the form of an elongated ring some 420 feet in length and 20 feet wide. Originally, the kiln was divided into 22 chambers, with one chamber at a time used to burn the lime. The chambers would be fired in sequence and it would take six weeks to complete one circuit. A walk around the kiln today is an eerie experience and not one for those afraid of dark confined spaces.

The lime works were once the site of a bitter industrial dispute. In 1901, men employed at the works joined the Leeds branch of the Gasworkers' and General Labourers' Union. On 6 September, 1902, 93 of these men were paid off and told they would no longer be permitted onto the site or allowed to live in the company's houses. Their 'crime' was not substandard work but the fact that they'd joined a union, which was against the company's rules. Some of these men had worked at Craven for 30 years or more. The strike lasted over half a year and ultimately resulted in the company winning. Non-union workers were employed to replace the striking workers and production of lime started up again.

In 1931, the kiln was extinguished and the quarry shut; competition from elsewhere had made the works economically unviable. In 1939 the Craven Lime Works finally closed for good.

ADDRESS Off the B6479, Settle, North Yorkshire, BD24 9NU, www.visitsettle.co.uk
TIP Visit the delightful village of Langcliffe just five minutes south of the lime works. The village has been designated as a conservation area thanks to its largely unspoilt and historic character.

45 Feizor Celtic Wall

Ancient architecture

You don't have to go far in the Dales to come across a drystone wall. There is one, however, that is unique, mysterious and strangely uncelebrated. The Feizor Celtic Wall is found on moorland opposite Smearsett Scar. It is split into two sections, the longest of which is some 65 feet in length and five feet high and wide, and which is separated from the smaller section by a 130-foot gap. For some reason, the Ordnance Survey neglect to show the wall on their maps and so many people come across it purely by chance.

Like most boundary and field walls in the Dales, no mortar or cement was used in the construction of the Celtic Wall. That is where the similarity ends, for it is sturdier than your typical farm wall and the stones used are far chunkier. Another curious aspect of the wall is that it stands alone and does not appear to have been connected to any other structure. What is not known is who built it or why, though naturally various theories have been put forward over the years. Alfred Wainwright, in his book *Wainwright in the Limestone Dales*, wrote that the wall was obviously ancient and that its position high on a point overlooking the Happy Valley 'suggests a defensive use, to repel invaders', though he conceded that this 'is conjecture and it remains a mystery'.

What is unlikely is that the Celtic Wall had an agricultural purpose. Sheep folds and hogg houses are commonly found across the Dales. These are stone structures found on the fells that have been built by farmers to provide shelter for their sheep during the winter months. (A hogg is the name for a sheep that has been weaned but has not yet had its first shearing.) The Celtic Wall, however, provides little shelter for sheep as it doesn't face into the prevailing wind. This mystery over its origin and purpose does mean that it can be freely interpreted by anyone who comes across it. So why not pay the Celtic Wall a visit and see what you make of it.

ADDRESS Feizor, North Yorkshire, LA2 8DF, operation.banquets.goods **TIP** Take a short detour to Stainforth Force on the way to Feizor. In the autumn you may even spot salmon leaping up the waterfall on their way upriver to spawn.

46 Pen-y-ghent

Pennine waypoint

In 1935, journalist Tom Stephenson wrote an article for the *Daily Herald* entitled 'Wanted – A Long Green Trail'. The trail, Stephenson argued, should be 'a Pennine Way from the Peak to the Cheviots'. This was a radical stance to take at the time. Landowners were noisily opposed to the general public tramping across their land and often took measures to prevent this. Stephenson's article was also published a mere three years after a mass trespass of Kinder Scout in the Peak District; the event was organised to highlight the injustice many felt at being denied access to England's open spaces.

It took 30 years of hard work and some intensive and occasionally bad-tempered negotiations for Stephenson's 'Pennine Way' to come into being, the new long-distance route opening on 24 April, 1965, precisely 33 years after the Kinder Scout protest. Sixty years later, the Pennine Way still starts at Edale in the Peak District, winding its way northwards up the 'spine of England' to conclude 268 miles later at Kirk Yetholm in the Scottish Borders.

Pen-y-ghent is on the route of the Pennine Way, and it's a popular walk for day trippers too. It's 2,227 feet high and very steep in places. If you're not attempting the entire Pennine Way then the simplest place to start your walk to the summit is Horton-in-Ribblesdale. If you follow the Pennine Way from the village you'll pass Hull Pot *en route*. This is a shakehole, the local name for a sinkhole. Hull Pot is roughly 300 feet long, 60 feet wide and 60 feet deep and is the largest natural hole in England.

Pen-y-ghent's distinctive stepped shape has been described as similar to a crouching lion, a loaf and the prow of a boat. The peak is also known as 'the hill of the winds' (you'll find out why at the top!). Just like Ingleborough and Whernside, Pen-y-ghent is Carboniferous limestone with a cap of millstone grit. Fittingly, it's grit you'll need to complete the entire Pennine Way.

ADDRESS The summit of Pen-y-ghent is marked by an OS trig point at covertly.replaces.fools TIP Refresh yourself after your adventure on Pen-y-ghent at the Blind Beck Tearoom in Horton-in-Ribblesdale (www.blindbeck.co.uk).

47 Georgian Sundials

Richmond has its time in the sun

Everyone needs a sundial in their life. Probably. A house in Richmond has two. One is on a wall facing east and works until midday(ish), after which the wall is in shadow. Fortunately, you can still tell the time by moving around the corner to the south-facing sundial. This sundial will then display the correct time for most of the rest of the afternoon. Unless it's cloudy, of course. In which case neither works very well. The east-facing sundial was made (or Fecit) in 1720 and sports the clever legend '*Ut Hora Sic Vita*' or 'As is the hour, so is life'. The south-facing sundial is one year younger. Both bear the name of their (obviously proud) maker – William Hutton – who lived in the house at the time.

Richmond had a good 18th century. The Georgian period saw the town boom economically and many fine buildings were built then. This is reflected in the number of listed buildings from this time that still stand. These include a good number of houses, a typical example of which was advertised in the *Newcastle Courant* on 20 May, 1727, as 'a good house, with all Conveniencies of Malting, Stables, with several Parcels of Ground'. If this sounds promising then you need to get in touch with a 'Mr. Gregory Elsley, or Mr. Marmaduke Theakston near Richmond'. It's entirely possible that they are no longer taking enquiries, however.

Arguably the most interesting remnant of 18th-century Richmond is the Georgian Theatre Royal on Victoria Road, built in 1788 by actor-manager Samuel Butler and his wife Tryphosa. The building was in use as a theatre until 1848 when it was let as an auction house. By the 1950s the interior was dilapidated and so in 1960 a non-profit trust to save the building was incorporated. The theatre was rescued, restored and re-opened in 1963. It is now Britain's oldest working theatre in its original form and is well worth a visit, even if you have to make time to do so.

ADDRESS The Green/Bridge Street, Richmond, North Yorkshire, DL10 4RG, www.richmond.org TIP The nearby Culloden Tower was built to commemorate the victory of the Duke of Cumberland over Bonnie Prince Charlie at Culloden in 1746

48 The Obelisk

*

Like many towns in Yorkshire, Richmond has a market square. And, in common with those other market squares, there is a 'cross' at the centre of Richmond's. What makes Richmond's market cross so unusual is its sheer size; it dominates the space and can't be missed, even when surrounded by market stalls.

Despite the name, market crosses aren't necessarily cross-shaped (though many are). Richmond's cross, known locally as the Obelisk, is a tall but narrow six-sided pillar topped with a stone ball. It was commissioned in 1771 by Richmond's then mayor, Christopher Wayne, to replace a far smaller medieval cross. The original cross was by all accounts very handsome indeed.

In *The History of Richmond* (1821), author Christopher Clarkson noted that an antiquary had described the first cross as 'the greatest beauty in the Town'. It was enclosed by 'a wall about six-feet high, in the form of a square', the four sides of which were 'enriched with many curious Gothic compartments and other ornamental designs'. The cross featured the arms of Fitz-Hugh, Scrope, Conier and Neville. And jauntily placed at each corner was 'a dog sitting made of stone'. The Obelisk is a far more restrained affair – austere even – a style typical of Georgian architecture.

Below the Obelisk and market square is a 12,000-gallon reservoir that was once used to supply Richmond with fresh water. According to Clarkson, people in the town originally drew their water 'from wells in various places, as from Nun's Well, and from that in the Friary'. The first attempt at an engineering solution occurred in 1583, when a pipeline (the pipes made from lime wood) was laid between Aislabeck springs to a wellhead in the market square. The 18th-century reservoir was far more ambitious and water was 'conveyed by pipes with public cocks to various parts of the town for the use of the inhabitants'.

ADDRESS Market Place, Richmond DL10 4QN, North Yorkshire, www.richmond.org **TIP** Richmond's varied and interesting outdoor market is held every Wednesday and Saturday.

49 Ripon Cathedral

St Wilfrid founds a church

If you pay a visit to the crypt below the Cathedral Church of St Peter and St Wilfrid (or Ripon Cathedral if you prefer) you will experience something akin to time travel. This narrow but very atmospheric underground catacomb was built in A.D. 672 and is the oldest extant structure in any English cathedral. The man responsible for the crypt and for founding the first church on the site of the current cathedral was St Wilfrid, who was born some 40 years earlier in the Kingdom of Northumbria.

St Wilfrid was something of a religious whirlwind. He was only 30 when he was made the Abbot of Ripon and Bishop of York. And he was more than happy to throw his intellectual weight around when it came to matters of doctrine. It was Wilfrid who, at the Synod of Whitby in A.D. 663–64, persuaded English Christians to follow the practices of Rome rather than those of the Celtic churches on Iona and Lindisfarne. St Wilfrid's victory may sound unimportant but (for one thing) it still determines when we celebrate Easter some 1,360 or so years later.

The church that St Wilfrid founded in Ripon was destroyed in A.D. 948. The current structure – the fourth to be built on the site – was begun in the 13th century at the instigation of Archbishop Roger de Pont l'Evêque. Over the centuries the church evolved as new details were added. Occasionally things were lost too. In 1450, an earthquake (or possibly a very heavy storm) caused the central crossing tower to collapse. During the English Civil War, Parliamentarians caused considerable damage to the cathedral. Soldiers smashed stained glass and destroyed carvings and effigies that they deemed idolatrous. Fortunately, the men left the carved wooden misericords in the choir stalls alone. These depict animals and fantastic figures, and are said to have inspired characters in Lewis Carroll's *Alice's Adventures in Wonderland*.

ADDRESS Minster Road, Ripon, North Yorkshire, HG4 1QT, +44 (0)1765 603462, www.riponcathedral.org.uk TIP Enjoy a few hours in Ripon's Spa Gardens. While you're there look out for a wonderful wooden sculpture featuring characters from *Alice in Wonderland*.

50 The Workhouse Museum

It's a gruel world

In the summer of 1945 the British people voted in a Labour government led by Clement Attlee. The new regime was elected after it promised to implement the recommendations of the *Social Insurance and Allied Services (Cmd. 6404)* report of 1942 (better known as the *Beveridge Report* after its author, William Beveridge). The paper had proposed a comprehensive reform of the country's welfare system to eradicate 'Want, Disease, Ignorance, Squalor and Idleness'. And so, in a series of Acts of Parliament, the government introduced the modern welfare system. One of these acts also repealed the Poor Law Amendment Act of 1834.

It's hard to believe how terrible the lives of Britain's poor were in the 19th century. Those on the poverty line faced the terrifying prospect of ending up in a workhouse. These were institutions that provided food and shelter in exchange for hard labour. They were deliberately designed to be harsh, cheerless places and run by people with little sympathy for the inmates. The hero of *Oliver Twist* starts his adventure in a workhouse, and George Orwell wrote of a night spent in one in *Down and Out in Paris and London*.

Although workhouses had existed before 1834, the Poor Law 'refined' how they were run. The law specified that men and women be kept separate, which often resulted in families being split apart. The inmates also had to wear a uniform at all times and they were not allowed to talk to one another during their stay.

The first workhouse in Ripon opened in 1776 and was able to accommodate 30 people. A new workhouse was built in 1854 on the same site, designed by William Perkin and Elisha Backhouse. Inmates shared the space with a teacher, doctors and a chaplain. They were expected to chop wood, do laundry and help tend the vegetables. The building now houses a splendid museum that tells the story of how Britain's poor fared in less enlightened times.

ADDRESS Workhouse Museum, Allhallowgate, Ripon, North Yorkshire, HG4 1LE, +44 (0)1765 690799, www.riponmuseums.co.uk TIP Learn more about law and order in historic Ripon by visiting the Prison & Police and Courthouse Museums (www.riponmuseums.co.uk).

51 Brigflatts Meeting House

'I have called you friends'

Life in the period during and immediately after the English Civil War was unsettled and febrile. Unnerving new ideas about how the nation could be shaped for the better began to proliferate. One group of people with a radically different concept of religion was George Fox's Religious Society of Friends. Fox and his preachers toured northern England proclaiming a more personal connection with God, that there was no need for an established church and that rituals and holy days were an unnecessary irrelevance. The preachers talked of the 'inner light', the voice of God that anyone could experience regardless of their place in the pecking order.

The Society of Friends are better known today as the Quakers. There are several possibilities for how the unusual name came about. One is that it was a description of the way that believers quivered with excitement when they thought they were in the presence of God. Another is that Fox told a judge that he should 'tremble at the word of the Lord'.

The first Quakers were persecuted and many were imprisoned for their beliefs. Despite this (and the Conventicle Act of 1670 that banned non-conformist meetings) Quakerism took hold in Yorkshire. Evidence for this is Brigflatts Meeting House near Sedbergh, built in 1675. It is the second-oldest purpose-built Friends Meeting House in England (Hertford Meeting House is older by five years). Constructed in a vernacular style, Brigflatts still retains most of the original interior oak furnishings and is rightly regarded as a place of peace and tranquillity by visitors.

Arguably even more affecting than Brigflatts is the nearby Quaker Burial Ground. A former apple orchard, the burial ground predates Brigflatts; Rebecca Langle was the first Friend to be buried there in 1656. In deference to the Quaker Equality Testimony, the headstones are all the same size and shape.

ADDRESS Brigflatts Lane, Sedbergh, Cumbria, LA10 5HN, www.brigflatts.org
TIP On 13 June, 1652, George Fox preached to a huge crowd from a craggy outcrop of rock now known as Fox's Pulpit near Firbank Fell. The meeting is regarded as the foundational event of the Quaker movement (threaded.threaten.occur).

52 Cautley Spout

Wheeeeeeee!

Record-breaking geographical features are relatively common in the Yorkshire Dales. You do occasionally have to be *very* specific when describing how a feature breaks a record, however. A good example is Cautley Spout in the Howgill Fells, which – at 650 feet – is England's highest *cascade* waterfall *above* ground. This is different from Hardraw Force and Gaping Gill, both of which boast longer *unbroken* falls – the former above ground, the latter plunging into the dark interior of a pothole. Happily, all three waterfalls are in the Yorkshire Dales so the region gets all the glory regardless.

Cautley Spout is formed by the convergence of a number of streams, all of which have their source on a high plateau known as The Calf. The waterfall tumbles down a narrow gully in a steep cliff face in a series of steps until it reaches the bottom of a glacial valley. At this point Cautley Spout becomes the less tumultuous Cautley Holme Beck, a tributary of the river Rawthey – a relatively minor watercourse that eventually flows into the river Lune south of Sedbergh. Although you can't follow Cautley Spout precisely there is a steep path that leads to the top of the falls and from which you can generally get a good view of the waterfall.

The Howgill Fells are visually and geographically different from the limestone landscapes found elsewhere in the Yorkshire Dales; the softly rounded hills were described poetically and rather accurately by outdoor writer Alfred Wainwright as resembling a 'herd of sleeping elephants'. The hills are formed from beds of sandstone, mudstone and siltstone, laid down during the Silurian Period some 440–420 million years ago. This was a time when life first began to colonise the land in the form of primitive plants and early types of spider. However, one striking aspect of the Howgills today is how treeless they are; trees only manage to survive on the bleak slopes in sheltered ravines and gills.

ADDRESS Sedbergh, Cumbria, LA10 5NE, www.yorkshiredales.org.uk, clauses.publisher.tabs **TIP** Continue on the steep path to join the route to the summit of The Calf. At 2,218 feet in height, this is the highest peak in the Howgill Fells.

53 Cross Keys Inn

No danger of a hangover

Don't head to the Cross Keys Inn if you fancy a pint or a glass of wine. You can get a perfectly satisfying tea or coffee and any amount of pop but not an alcoholic drink. The inn is proudly temperance when it comes to serving intoxicating liquor, though you are more than welcome to bring your own if you're eating there (the landlord will happily provide the glasses).

The Cross Keys Inn was originally a farmhouse known as High Haygarth. Records show that a Thomas Bland was living there in 1619, so parts of the building are very old indeed. Confusingly, a date on a door lintel seems to suggest that the farmhouse was built in 1732, though this probably records the year that the building underwent major renovation or rebuilding. The initials HJA are also carved into the lintel and they refer to the owners of High Haygarth at the time, John and Agnes Howgill. The farmhouse was converted into an inn sometime after 1819 when the route of the Cautley road was altered to pass by High Haygarth.

The inn stopped selling alcohol after an unfortunate accident following a night of enthusiastic drinking. The story told is that a local man – with the family name of Buck – left at the end of the evening for the walk back to Ravenstonedale. Fearing that Buck was a danger to himself, the landlord decided to accompany him home. The landlord was right to worry for Buck tumbled down the banks of the river Rawthey. Trying to help the man, the poor landlord fell into the river and was drowned. On 27 October, 1902, the inn was sold at auction to Mrs Sarah Buck, who then sold it on to Mrs Edith Adelaide Bunney. It was Edith who removed the liquor licence and the inn has not sold a drop of alcohol in all the years since.

Cross Keys Inn was bequeathed to the National Trust in 1949, and they own it to this day. This means that the future of the inn is secure, which is something we can all raise a non-alcoholic glass to.

ADDRESS Cautley, Sedbergh, Cumbria, LA10 5NE, +44 (0)1539 620284, www.cautleyspout.co.uk **TIP** See the work of local artists and craftspeople at Farfield Mill on the river Clough near Sedbergh (www.farfieldmill.org).

54 Sedbergh

Scholarly

The town of Sedbergh has a long and distinguished history. It is first mentioned officially in the Domesday Book, the exhaustive survey of England and parts of Wales compiled on the orders of Norman King William in 1086. Curiously, Sedbergh had no recorded population at the time and was described as 'waste' and so no taxes were due. This is possibly because Sedbergh was destroyed in 1069 during William's brutal subjugation of northern England, known to history as the 'Harrying of the North'.

Sedbergh had obviously bounced back by 1525 for this was the year that Roger Lupton founded Sedbergh School. Local legend has it that the young Lupton walked the 300 or so miles to London from Sedbergh in order to gain an education and to better himself. Although this is unlikely to be true, Lupton *did* do well for himself. Over the course of his long life, he served as chaplain to King Henry VII and Henry VIII, and was Provost of Eton College for more than 30 years. Lupton's school was initially a single room affair and was run with the aim of 'maintaining and increase of learning in Christ's Church' and as Lupton later wrote 'for my soul's health'. The school has expanded considerably since Lupton's day and is now regarded as one of the top boarding schools in the world.

Lupton revered learning and so would have been delighted when Sedbergh was named England's Book Town. The early years of the 21st century were not good to Sedbergh, however. The 2001 outbreak of foot and mouth disease resulted in fewer summer visitors to the town. There were three bookshops in Sedbergh at the time so a committee (the Area Actions for Sedbergh Initiative) was formed to pursue the idea of becoming a book town. After various events and studies, with funding from the likes of the Yorkshire Dales National Park and Rural Regeneration Cumbria, the dream came true with the town's first Book Festival in the late summer of 2005.

ADDRESS Sedbergh, Cumbria, www.sedbergh.org.uk **TIP** Look out for the various sheep-themed activities in Sedbergh every August during Sheepfest (www.sheepfest.co.uk).

55 Attermire Scar

Limestone attraction

Attermire Scar is a rolling series of limestone cliffs pockmarked with caves. The origin of the scar has long intrigued people. An article by Jerry Daffelem for the *Intelligencer Supplement,* published on 20 September, 1856, is a typical example of this fascination. Daffelem poetically (and correctly) described how the scar was formed underwater and that 'where we stand giant fishes once roved, and crystal waves made music over beds of corals and fairy-like shells'. Daffelem also wrote that the 'occurrence of bones in the caves of Craven was a fact known years ago, though little curiosity seems to have been awakened as to how they had got there'.

The bones Daffelem described were those of spotted hyenas, elephants, hippos and lions, discovered in the caves earlier in the 19th century. These are relatively young geologically speaking and date from roughly 120,000 years ago when Yorkshire was considerably warmer. Daffelem did lament that people did not believe the antiquity of the bones, believing that they were left there by 'ancient banditti, who made these caves their country quarters'.

The largest cave on the scar is Victoria Cave. It was discovered in 1837 by tinsmith Michael Horner, who was out on the fells with his dogs. One of the dogs happened to chase a fox into a small hole. When the dog failed to return, Horner dug out sediment to enlarge the hole and crawled inside. Grubbing around he found Romano-British coins on the cave floor. Horner mentioned the discovery to his boss, Joseph Jackson, who was an amateur archaeologist. The pair returned to the cave on 28 June, 1838, the day of Queen Victoria's coronation, to explore further. Being patriotic, Jackson named the cave after the nation's new monarch. A larger entrance to the cave was later created to allow easier access and it soon became a popular tourist attraction. Sadly, it is now deemed too dangerous for visitors and so has been closed to the public.

ADDRESS Settle, North Yorkshire, BD24 9NF, www.yorkshiredales.org.uk TIP Have a bite to eat at the wonderfully named Ye Olde Naked Man Café in Settle (www.yeoldenakedmancafe.com).

56 Castleberg Rock

Look down on Settle

If you want to find your way around Settle with confidence then you could do a whole lot worse than walk to the summit of Castleberg Rock first. From the top you can see virtually the whole of the town and its street layout, as well as across the river Ribble to Giggleswick and the hills of the Forest of Bowland beyond.

Castleberg Rock has been a popular tourist attraction since the early 18th century. A sketch by artist Samuel Buck made in 1720 shows that the rock had been put to good use too. According to an edition of the *Yorkshire Post* printed in October 1932, the summit of Castleberg Rock once 'formed a gnomon of a crude but impressive sun-dial, the shadow of which passed over five flat stones on the lower slopes and showed the time to the inhabitants of the surrounding district'. Don't go looking for the cunning craggy clock now, however. It was removed in the early 19th century and replaced with the current path. However, there are some who think that the sundial only ever existed in Buck's imagination.

The rock has given the good folk of Settle a scare or two in the past. In 1883, two large stones came loose from the cliff, one of which crashed through a wall behind the town's Congregational Chapel and damaged the choir window. The other, estimated to weigh a ton and a half at the time, tumbled into the yard behind the National School. Fortunately, no one was hurt in the event.

The path is by far the easiest way to reach the summit but – if you're that way inclined! – you can also climb your way to the top. The British Mountaineering Council lists a number of different routes up the face of the crag, many of which have charming names, such as 'Poppies for Tea?' and 'Ye Olde Naked Man'. Other names are slightly more worrying. There has to be a story to 'Settle Injuries Clinic' and 'Shock Treatment', for example. Perhaps 'Scary Mary' failed to provide 'Spot-on, Health and Safety'?

ADDRESS Castlebergh Lane, Settle, North Yorkshire, BD24 9ET, www.visitsettle.co.uk, layered.reinstate.from **TIP** Settle Market was granted a charter by King Henry III in 1249; it is now held every Tuesday in the Market Place.

57 The Flowerpot Festival

Flobbadob

A flowerpot is an everyday object, something you would never normally take much notice of unless you needed one. However, wander round Settle in July and August and you won't be able to miss them. They are everywhere. That said, most of them are cunningly camouflaged so you may not recognise them as actual flowerpots. You'll see them dressed up as well-known cartoon characters, animals or celebrities. You may even spot flowerpots dressed as people indulging in wholesome activities, such as fishing or just relaxing on benches watching the world go by. But don't worry. You're not imagining things. You are taking part in Settle's wonderfully eccentric and uplifting annual Flowerpot Festival.

The idea for the festival was planted in the mind of organiser, Steve Amphlett, during a family holiday in a west country village sometime in the early 1990s. It was there that Steve saw flowerpot displays and spent a happy few hours wandering around the village, 'flowerpot spotting' with his children. The concept leapt to mind in 2014 when Steve, along with the team at Vibrant Settle, were trying to think of a suitably jolly theme for a proposed festival.

The eminently sensible goal of the first Flowerpot Festival was to create a delightfully quirky event that would bring the whole community together in a fun and inclusive way, and that would also have the useful side-effect of encouraging people from outside the area to visit the town (who would then spend money in local shops and cafés, of course). Happily, the first festival – and every festival since – has achieved exactly that.

Steve and the good folk of Vibrant Settle are delighted with how the festival has been embraced by the town. As Steve describes it 'the festival has succeeded beyond our wildest dreams, is now a proud fixture in the Settle calendar and attracts visitors from all over the country (and some overseas visitors!)'.

ADDRESS Flowerpot Trails with suggested routes around Settle are available locally for a small fee, www.settleflowerpotfestival.co.uk TIP Have a pint and hear live music at the family-run Talbot Arms in Settle (www.talbotsettle.co.uk).

58 The Folly

Actually useful

Don't be fooled by the name. The Folly in Settle is a wonderful old building just a few minutes' walk from the centre of town. It was built in the 1670s by Richard Preston, a wealthy local lawyer, as a home for him, his wife Lettice and their three daughters, Margaret, Millicent and Lettice. Richard, ironically for a lawyer, died without a will in 1695. This complicated matters and it wasn't until 1702 that the ownership of the Folly passed to Margaret. However, she quickly sold the property on to Margaret Dawson, who bought it for her son William. It is at this point that the history of the building really becomes more complicated.

William Dawson never lived in the Folly. He had recently inherited Langcliffe Hall, a few miles north of Settle, and decided to live there instead. And so the Folly was divided into separate spaces that were let as apartments and to a variety of businesses. Some of the businesses run from the Folly included a furniture shop, a bank, a bakery (run in the 1840s by Jane Ingham, who specialised in oatcakes known locally as havercakes), a potato wholesaler, and even a fish and chip shop. The latter business was owned in the early 1900s by David Hearsum with his wife Isabella, whose surname before marriage was (rather wonderfully) Fryer.

Phillip Dawson was the last in his family to own the Folly. When he inherited it, the Folly was in a dilapidated state. Phillip did much to restore the building during his ownership of it. However, he sold the building in 1983 to a local antiques dealer, though he hoped that one day the building would house a museum.

In 1996, the North Craven Building Preservation Trust bought part of the Folly. Five years later, Prince Charles opened the charming and informative Museum of North Craven Life, fulfilling Philip's dream. Happily, the trust were able to buy the rest of the building in 2010 and so the Folly is now entirely in their care.

ADDRESS Victoria Street, Settle, North Yorkshire, BD24 9EY, +44 (0)1729 825185, www.thefolly.org.uk **TIP** Go for a walk along the banks of the river Ribble west of Settle and look out for the Giggleswick Memorial Bridge commemorating the sacrifices made by Britain's armed services since 1914.

59 Gallery on the Green

Standing room only

The mobile phone has changed life for ever. Virtually everyone has one and so making a call to friends or family has never been so easy or so convenient. It really isn't long ago, however, that, for many, the neighbourhood phone box was the only way to stay in touch telephonically. Now telephone boxes are largely surplus to requirements and are slowly disappearing from urban centres and rural locations. Is this a bad thing? The modern glass and aluminium BT phone boxes (the KX series) will probably fade into history with few mourning their passing. The same cannot be said of the iconic (K6) red phone box, however.

The K6 made its first appearance in 1935 and was created to mark the Silver Jubilee of King George V. It was designed by noted architect Sir Giles Gilbert Scott, who also worked on the designs of Liverpool Cathedral and Bankside Power Station. Scott's telephone box was immediately popular with the public. By the time the last one was manufactured in 1968, over 60,000 had been installed across the country. Curiously, the only contentious aspect of the K6 was the colour. Scott himself thought that the K6 should be painted a 'toned white' or a 'warm, dove grey'. In 1936, Hubert Thornley, clerk for the North Riding of Yorkshire, fumed in a letter to his MP that the red paint was 'like an evil deed in a good world'. From 1946, the GPO allowed some phone boxes in areas of special beauty to be painted a less strident grey.

Most of the K6 phones are long gone, replaced by the KX or removed altogether. Happily, some remain *in situ* and are being put to other uses. This has been the lucky fate of the phone box on Green Head Lane in Settle. Since 2009, this particular box has been home to the Gallery on the Green, thought to be the smallest public art gallery in the world. A regular programme of exhibitions has kept people engaged ever since.

ADDRESS Green Head Lane, Settle, North Yorkshire, BD24 9HL, www.galleryonthegreen.org.uk, intend.showcases.arranger TIP Enjoy a carefully curated collection of crafts, jewellery and art at Studio Vault (www.studiovault.co.uk).

60 Victoria Hall

Enter stage right

Settle's glorious Victoria Hall is the oldest surviving music hall in the world, first opening its doors on 11 October, 1853. The event was described in an article in the *Leeds Intelligencer* 11 days later. The author of the piece correctly predicted that the new venue would 'contribute so much to the instruction and entertainment of the inhabitants of Settle and its neighbourhood', and that 'no expense seems to have been spared'.

The opening of the hall began with a festival of classical music, starting with a performance of the *The Creation* by Haydn. This was sung by members of the Settle Choral Society with assistance from the Leeds Choral Society, and by 'several distinguished vocalists whose services had been specially engaged for the occasion'. The reporter from the *Leeds Intelligencer* thoroughly enjoyed the evening and wrote that 'there was nothing to be desired in reference to this performance'. However, there were 'several empty seats in the area of the hall, which ought to have been filled'.

Music hall was a Victorian invention. An evening's entertainment would be varied and include rousing popular songs and acrobatics, as well as comic turns. In the 1850s music halls were being built across the entire nation. By 1875 there were some 375 music halls in the Greater London area alone. Music hall also led to the rise of the first 'superstars'. Marie Lloyd was one of the biggest names in Britain in the 1890s; known as the 'Queen of the Music Halls', she was beloved by the public both for her singing and for her slightly cheeky use of barely concealed innuendo.

Victoria Hall was built thanks to the Revd James Robinson, himself an active member of the Settle Choral Society. Robinson paid for the construction of the building 'in a spirit of praiseworthy liberality'. In 1921, the hall was donated by the Robinson family to Craven District Council.

ADDRESS Kirkgate, Settle, North Yorkshire, BD24 9DZ, +44 (0)1729 825718, www.settlevictoriahall.org.uk TIP Named after the irrepressible *Countdown* host, the Richard Whiteley Theatre is a new arts venue in Giggleswick, developed and run by the village's school (richardwhiteleytheatre.giggleswick.org.uk).

61 Billy Bob's Parlour

Party like it's 1959

Diners are a true American institution. The first modern diners were opened in the 1920s, often in converted railway cars. The invention of the pre-fabricated diner that could be delivered anywhere there was a suitable space made them simple and relatively inexpensive to open. And so diners spread to every corner of the US, often near freeway intersections and in busy urban areas. Today, although franchised fast food restaurants have taken a toll on their numbers, diners are still an important and much-loved part of US life.

Diners have definitely left their mark in art. Edward Hopper's *Nighthawks*, painted in 1942, offers a bleak but curiously fascinating vision of an urban diner at night. However, it is in movies where you're most likely to see a diner. Sometimes diners play host to criminals and lowlifes: *Taxi Driver* and *Pulp Fiction*, for example. But more often they are a place of fun and laughter: *Muppets Take Manhattan* and *When Harry Met Sally* both show diners at their wholesome best. And then there's the bittersweet *Diner* in which a diner (surprise!) plays a prominent role.

The UK has long had tea shops and cafés, and so diners never really caught on here. Wonderfully, however, you can find a thoroughly American diner tucked away in a quiet corner of the Yorkshire Dales. Step into Billy Bob's Parlour and you are instantly transported back to the 1950s. The decor is authentic, the pop music catchy and era appropriate, and the menu is replete with classic diner favourites (or should that be favorites?). There is even a big yellow school bus neatly parked in one corner of the parlour.

Billy Bob's Parlour was the brainchild of Mandy and Gary Rogers, who opened the diner in 2011. The couple are so keen to create the right ambience that they regularly travel to the US to source new decor. Thanks to their efforts, Billy Bob's is so authentically American that you may forget to drive on the left when you leave.

ADDRESS Calm Slate Farm, Halton East, Bolton Abbey, North Yorkshire, BD23 6EU, +44 (0)1756 711826, www.billybobsparlour.com **TIP** If you need to burn off the calories then the short but satisfying walk to Embsay Crag (headers.playing.backdrop) from Embsay Reservoir will do the trick.

62 The Embsay & Bolton Abbey Steam Railway

You'll be chuffed

The busy towns of Skipton and Ilkley aren't that far apart as the crow flies; you can drive between the two in 20 minutes or so. Life is more complicated if you want to catch the train, however. Starting from Skipton, you first need to catch a train all the way to Shipley where you then change for the service to Ilkley. Even if all goes well it won't take less than three-quarters of an hour. Look on a map at the long looping route and you can see why. After scratching your head for a while you may then wonder why there isn't a more direct link between the two settlements. Would it surprise you to discover that there once was? The wonderful Embsay & Bolton Abbey Steam Railway is all that is now left of this long-gone line.

The Skipton-Ilkley railway opened on 1 October, 1888, and was commissioned and run by Midland Railways. The very first through ticket was sold to a Welbury Kendall, a successful timber merchant from Skipton. During its history, the line was often used by the Duke of Devonshire, who owned Bolton Hall in Wharfedale. The duke owned grouse moors so reigning kings and queens were frequent visitors and often used the railway too (as far as is known, the final visit of the Royal Train was October 1947). The line was also popular with workers visiting Bolton Abbey from factory towns in both Yorkshire and Lancashire. However, *they* probably weren't allowed on the duke's grouse moors.

The end came in March 1965 when the line was closed following publication of the *Beeching Report* into Britain's railways. Fortunately, the story didn't end there. The Embsay & Grassington Railway Preservation Society was formed in 1968. Although the whole line could not be resurrected, the (renamed) Yorkshire Dales Railway Museum Trust now offers a thrilling and nostalgic steam service between Embsay and Bolton Abbey stations.

ADDRESS Embsay Station, Off East Lane, Embsay, Skipton, North Yorkshire, BD23 6QX, or Bolton Abbey Station, Bolton Abbey, Skipton, North Yorkshire, BD23 6AF, +44 (0)1756 710614, www.embsayboltonabbeyrailway.org.uk **TIP** Skipton Castle woods is an ancient woodland dating back to the 10th century (skipton.woodlandtrust.org.uk).

63 Little Theatre

'All the world's a stage'

The Skipton Players have been regularly entertaining the town of Skipton for more than 90 years. Although the exact date of formation is now lost, archive material shows that the Players performed *The Barretts of Wimpole Street* by Rudolf Besier at Skipton's Town Hall in 1934. Curiously, the Skipton Players were originally known as the Skipton and District Amateur Operatic and Dramatic Society, and were one of two groups in the town with that name. A notice in the *Yorkshire Post* on 5 May, 1934, announced that the duplication 'has [understandably] caused confusion in the mind of the public and certain misunderstandings have resulted'. With the sensible name change effected, the group's secretary hoped that 'both societies will continue to support each other's productions'.

For 26 years the Players continued to perform with aplomb in the Town Hall. In November 1938, the Players won the Irving Trophy at the fourth Craven Drama Festival for their 'excellent performance' of *Love on the Dole* by Ronald Gow and Walter Greenwood. And their first war-time production was *When We Are Married* by J. B. Priestley, performed in May 1940, in which Charles Rushforth 'revelled in the role of the tipsy press photographer'.

What the Players really desired was a permanent home of their own. This wish came true in 1959. For a very reasonable £250, the Players bought a former stables that had more recently been used as an antique dealer's storeroom. Conversion of the property took almost a year, with the cost eventually totalling £2,000. The first production in the new Little Theatre was *The Mayor of Tarentelle*.

The Little Theatre is aptly named. The auditorium is only 28 feet long and can seat just 70 people. The stage itself is 13 feet wide and a mere four feet from the front row. However, as Mary Wales – the architect who designed the theatre – pointed out in an interview with the *Yorkshire Post*, 'it's a bit Heath Robinson, but it works'.

ADDRESS Clifford Street, Skipton, North Yorkshire, BD23 2AD, +44 (0)1756 802177, www.skiptonlittletheatre.org.uk **TIP** Take a step back in time by visiting the 900-year-old Skipton Castle (www.skiptoncastle.co.uk).

64 Rylstone Cross

Celebrating peace

The Napoleonic Wars of the late 18th and early 19th centuries were a fraught time for the United Kingdom. France, under the military leadership of Napoleon Bonaparte, was a constant threat. For nearly 20 years, invasion by sea was a very real possibility. Fighting the French proved a massive drain on Britain's economy too. As a result, we have Napoleon to thank for income tax. This unpopular levy – introduced in 1799 – was needed to pay back the national debt, which had ballooned due to the wars.

Fortunately, Napoleon was finally defeated at the Battle of Waterloo on 18 June, 1815. He surrendered to the British soon afterwards and was promptly banished to the remote volcanic island of St Helena in the South Atlantic. The plucky Brits then celebrated the end to hostilities in a number of different ways, including building monuments in some very odd places.

One of these curious memorials is the Rylstone Cross, erected on Hall Fell in 1822 – the year after Napoleon expired in exile. Or more accurately, the Rylstone Pillar, sculpted out of local rock by the menfolk of the village, was created then. The pillar became a cross in 1887 to celebrate Victoria's Golden Jubilee. The arms of the cross were made from wood and were attached to the pillar with some nifty braces made from iron.

Wood of course rots when left out in the elements. After 30 years exposed to moorland weather, the arms eventually fell off. Two joiners, Eric and Norman Clarke, were tasked with repairing the cross, which they did using a solid piece of oak. Jump forward to 1995 and the cross was once again in poor condition. So farmer Jim Caygill called on various companies to provide the materials for a new monument. Happily, Jim's powers of persuasion worked. A new three-tonne stone cross was made and airlifted into position. It is likely to remain a landmark for many years to come.

ADDRESS Hall Fell, North Yorkshire, BD23 6ER, staples.koala.cyber **TIP** St Peter's Church in Rylstone is a handsome Victorian Grade II-listed building.

65 Buttertubs Pass

Natural refrigeration

Getting from one dale to another usually requires taking a high road, otherwise known as a pass. These roads are not for the faint of heart or if you've just passed your driving test. They can be winding. They can be steep. And there may well be a sheer drop mere yards from the edge of the road. The upside is that the views can be tremendous if you're able to pull over safely and take a look.

Buttertubs Pass is the quintessential Dales pass. The road links Swaledale and Wensleydale and threads its way steeply up to a maximum elevation of 1,690 feet, passing between the peaks of Great Shunner Fell (the third highest summit in the Yorkshire Dales) and the wonderfully named Lovely Seat.

The pass is named after a cluster of very deep vertical potholes on the Swaledale side of the pass. It's said (though there's no definitive proof) that farmers on their way to market would stop to rest there. When the weather was warm, they would lower the butter they were hoping to sell into the cool depths of the potholes to stop it from melting, hence the name. Until relatively recently it was possible to stand at the edge of the Buttertubs. Now they have been cordoned off by a wooden safety fence, so you'll have to keep your butter (or vegan alternative) cool some other way.

Buttertubs Pass is (understandably) a popular route for motorists after a challenge. Remarkably, this was the case even in the 1930s, when car ownership was still uncommon. A writer for the *Daily Mail* noted in 1931 that 'the pass now has quite a good surface, and, though steep is practicable for motoring'. The writer concluded somewhat ominously that Buttertubs is 'not a road suitable for night driving, however'. Bad weather can occasionally close the pass. However, perhaps the most bizarre event that resulted in closure was a fire on a coach in 1985. Fortunately, the closure was temporary and no one was injured.

ADDRESS Buttertubs, Cliff Gate Road, Thwaite, North Yorkshire, DL11 6DR, www.yorkshiredales.org.uk, overhear.elder.avoiding **TIP** The B6255 between Ribblehead Viaduct and Hawes is considered to be one of the more challenging but rewarding routes in the Yorkshire Dales.

66 Crackpot Hall

A wild child of the fells?

The wonderfully named Crackpot Hall is a ruin now. It was built in the 18th century, though it probably replaced an earlier structure. The amusing (to modern ears) name is likely to derive from a combination of the Old English for crow ('crack') and the local word for cave ('pot'). What it certainly wasn't was a hall; it was used as a farmhouse until it was abandoned in the early 1950s after subsidence adversely affected its structure. What makes the ruin such a draw is entirely down to two rather special women.

Ella Pontefract and Marie Hartley wrote books about the Yorkshire Dales, starting with *Swaledale*, published in 1934. They also collected domestic items, as well as tools used by working men and women in the Dales. Their ultimately substantial collection eventually found its way to the splendid Dales Countryside Museum, where it can be seen to this day. Their partnership came to end with Ella's tragically early death in 1945.

One of the stories in *Swaledale* concerns Alice, a four-year-old girl they encountered near Crackpot Hall. After first snatching the authors' caps and sticks away, Alice clambers over a stone wall 'with a mocking, chuckling laugh'. She talks to Ella and Marie, but her dialect is so strong 'that it might be a foreign tongue'. Although Ella and Marie didn't describe her as such, the idea of a feral child on the fells of Swaledale took hold in the popular imagination.

In 2017, having long been intrigued by the story, author David Almond presented 'Alice at Crackpot Hall' for the BBC Radio 3 series *Between the Ears.* He posed the question 'Could Alice have really existed?' Wonderfully, after some deft detective work, the (then) 88-year-old Alice Harker was tracked down and interviewed in her home near Carlisle. Bright and cheerful, Alice recalled her fateful encounter with Ella and Marie for Almond; the author happily concluding that the 'wild child still survives in her'.

ADDRESS Near Keld, North Yorkshire, DL11 6LJ, doubt.slings.pleaser **TIP** Pay a visit to Kisdon Force while you're in the area (mountain.quietest.selling). This charming waterfall is an ideal place for a picnic too.

67 Drystone Barns and Walls

Defining the landscape

The distinctive stone barns of Swaledale (and the Dales generally) date back to the 18th and 19th centuries. Cattle, at this point in time, were more abundant in the Dales than they are now. The barns were used to store hay for the farmer's herd, as well as provide a warm shelter for the cattle during the winter months. There are still some 6,200 of these barns standing across the Dales, of which 1,000 or so can be found in Swaledale. The barns are often home to species like barn owls (of course), bats and, during the summer months, swallows and swifts.

The Yorkshire Dales are crisscrossed by attractive drystone walls, which add character to the landscape. There are roughly 5,000 miles of drystone walling in the Dales. This would get you to Vancouver in Canada if you were to walk directly west from the Dales. (Don't try this as the Atlantic Ocean gets in the way.) Exactly when it occurred to someone to create the very first drystone wall is now a mystery. However, the walls in the Dales largely date from the late 17th and early 18th century. This was during the time of the enclosure movement, when communal land was 'enclosed' by walls and hedgerow and taken into private hands. This process ultimately led to larger and more efficient farms. However, it also resulted in the dispossession of many poorer farmers and labourers, who until then had made their living on the land. Many of these men and women moved to cities such as Leeds and Bradford, where they sought work in the new factories of the Industrial Revolution.

Building and maintaining a drystone wall is time-consuming, and is an art that takes hours to master. Many farmers elsewhere in the county now prefer the ease of wire fencing. Fortunately, the drystone walls – as well as many barns – are protected through landscape conservation policies, keeping them safe for the future.

ADDRESS Drystone walls and barns can be found extensively across Swaledale and throughout the Yorkshire Dales TIP Find out more about the building of drystone walls from the Yorkshire Dry Stone Walling Guild and look out for their occasional training days in the Dales area (www.ydswg.co.uk).

68 Graculus Sculptures

Copper load of this

The human race has made use of many different kinds of metals over the millennia. The metal that helped humanity step deftly out of the Stone Age was copper. Copper has been used continuously for more than seven millennia in places such as the Middle East, India and North America. It's probable that copper was first used in its native state hewn directly from natural deposits. However, copper in this form is inconveniently brittle. Fortunately, someone discovered that heating copper first – a process known as annealing – makes it easier to hammer into shape. The next leap forward occurred when smelting was invented. This allowed the extraction of purer copper from ores such as chalcopyrite, as well as being able to pour the molten metal into moulds.

The modern world could not function without copper. Thanks to its high conductivity it is the metal that brings electricity to our homes. Because it is non-toxic and resists both heat and corrosion, copper is also used to make the pipes in our plumbing. And, rather wonderfully, it can also be used to make art.

Artist Michael Kusz has made (reclaimed) copper his material of choice in the creation of an on-going series of wonderfully imaginative sculptures. In his own words, it is 'a fantastic metal – versatile in the extreme. Stretch it, shrink it, cast it, electro-plate it, hammer it, punch it, it'll do anything you ask of it'. Michael particularly enjoys the range of colours that copper exhibits, especially the green of verdigris caused as copper oxidises.

Michael works from his studio – Graculus Sculptures – in Reeth, sharing the space with Joe, a very mischievous but friendly crow. His work is influenced by the forms and textures found in the natural world. The sculptures range in size from the huge to pieces you can hold in your hand (Michael's copper bats are exceptionally sweet). So plan a visit as soon as possible, ore you'll truly miss out.

ADDRESS Studio 6, Silver Street, Reeth, North Yorkshire, DL11 6SP, +44 (0)1748 884628, www.graculus.co.uk **TIP** Tuck in to home-cooked food at The Copper Kettle café on Anvil Square.

69 Ivelet Bridge

Humpbacked

There are a good number of wonderfully quaint stone structures in the Yorkshire Dales. Perhaps the most handsome of these is Ivelet Bridge on the river Swale, just five minutes' drive west from the village of Gunnerside. Built late in the 16th century, Ivelet Bridge was granted Grade II*-listed status in December 1966.

Ivelet Bridge is a packhorse bridge, originally built for traders taking goods to market by horse. This explains the narrowness of the road, which is a positively slender six feet from one side to the other. (This is a structure that was *not* designed with the motor car in mind.) It also explains the very low side walls or parapets. This is a common feature of this type of bridge as it reduced the risk that a low-slung pannier borne by a horse would catch on the parapet.

By far the most striking aspect of the bridge is the single arch that rises steeply but gracefully up and over the Swale. The arch is thought to be the highest of any stone bridge in the Yorkshire Dales. This also presents something of a hazard for the motorist. Ivelet Bridge is essentially a blind summit and so great care must be taken when attempting to drive over it. You really *don't* want to meet someone coming the other way at any speed.

A headless black dog allegedly haunts Ivelet Bridge. The spectral canine runs silently up to the top of the bridge, from where he (she?) leaps over the parapet wall and dives into the Swale. Seeing the horrible hound is far from ideal, and is said locally to be a portent of death. Perhaps not coincidentally, Ivelet Bridge is on the route of the original 16-mile Corpse Way between Keld and the churchyard in Grinton. On the north side of the bridge you can still see a flat rock known as a coffin stone. These are found all along the Corpse Way and are where pallbearers could set a coffin down while they rested for a few minutes or so. Or possibly less if a particularly menacing black dog happened to wander past.

ADDRESS Ivelet, North Yorkshire, DL11 6JQ, onlookers.senders.winters TIP Another quirky bridge on the river Swale is the Reeth Suspension Bridge. This is the second of two identical bridges; the first was destroyed during a flood in 2000 and replaced soon afterwards.

70 The Old Working Smithy

Testing 1... 2... 3...

Once upon a time, virtually every village in the country had a blacksmith. He (a smith was always male) made and repaired goods using iron or steel. If you needed a new hinge, a tool mending or a horse shod then the smith was the man for you. He was the essential cog that kept the rural economy turning. Now – thanks to mass production – blacksmiths are a rarity.

Gunnerside is one of those unusual villages that can still boast a smithy. The Old Working Smithy was established in the early 19th century. Remarkably, records kept at the smithy list every customer and job undertaken since 1840. These include the everyday work required of a smith (making horseshoes appears frequently), as well as one-off tasks such as the repair of a child's minnow net.

Look closely at the smith door and you'll see lots of curious marks and apparently random groups of letters. These are mainly sheep brands used to identify which farmer a particular sheep belonged to. This was important at a time when mixed herds of sheep were grazed on common land. Unlike cattle, sheep were branded on their horns and so the branding marks are far smaller. The marks on the door are where the smith tested his branding iron before putting it to use on the sheep. Farmers now use plastic ear tags, which is efficient and clinical but far less romantic.

The Calvert family has been in charge of the smithy for six generations, starting with John Calvert (born in 1782). The current owner is Stephen Calvert who, in 2003, turned part of the smithy into a fascinating museum where you can learn about the life of a village blacksmith. You may even see Stephen, who still works as a smith. Although he is more likely to be making decorative items rather than farm tools, it's good to know that there is a corner of Yorkshire where traditional skills are still forging ahead.

ADDRESS The Old Working Smithy, Rose Cottage, Gunnerside, North Yorkshire, DL11 6LE, +44 (0)1748 886577, www.gunnerside.info TIP The Kings Head is a friendly community-owned pub that boasts a good range of beers and spirits and an extensive, tempting menu (www.kingsheadgunnerside.com).

71 Swaledale Sheep

'Four legs good, two legs bad'

There are 15 national parks in the United Kingdom each with its own representative logo. Appropriately, the logo for the Yorkshire Dales National Park features a portrait of a Swaledale sheep. There are some 600,000 sheep in the park area, 30 times the number of people who live there. Not all these sheep are Swaledales but the breed is extremely common across the Dales, as well as in the neighbouring counties of Cumbria and County Durham.

Swaledales are popular because they are a hardy breed, well suited to the harsh weather often found in upland areas. Swaledale ewes are also renowned for being good, attentive mothers regardless of the weather. The breed's milk is prized and is used to make local cheeses. And Swaledale lamb and mutton are regarded as a delicacy, the meat being tender and full of flavour. Less well regarded is the off-white fleece, which is coarse and thick. Swaledale wool is typically used to make items that need to be durable such as carpets and rugs, or coats and other outerwear. As well as keeping the sheep warm, the fleece also quickly dries after a soaking. Wet sheep are top heavy and are prone to keeling over. Riggwelter is a Dales word that describes a sheep that has toppled over and needs human help to right itself. Thanks to its fleece, this undignified state of affairs is less likely to happen to a Swaledale.

The most distinctive feature of a Swaledale (grown by both ewes and tups) is its horns, which curl around the ears. The breed is also distinguished by a black face and white patches around the eyes and on the muzzle. Unlike a lot of other sheep breeds, the tail of Swaledales is not docked and grows long and woolly. The tail helps to protect the udders of ewes in cold weather, and also contains fat that is used in an emergency as a source of energy. Swaledales have been known to survive being trapped in deep snow for days or even weeks with the help of this useful reserve.

ADDRESS Swaledale sheep are commonly found on the fells and on farmland throughout the Yorkshire Dales **TIP** Look out for the far more rare Wensleydale breed of sheep, which have grey-black faces, ears and legs, and have thicker and softer fleeces than Swaledales.

72 Tan Hill Inn

Check the weather forecast

The Dales boast a number of record-breaking locations. One of those is Tan Hill Inn which, situated at an elevation of 1,732 feet, has the distinction of being the highest pub in the British Isles. It is 11 miles from the nearest town (Kirkby Stephen) and four miles from its nearest neighbour. The inn has its own ghost (ex-landlady Susan Peacock) and water supply, was first mentioned in print in 1586, and featured in an advert for double glazing in the 1980s.

Tan Hill Inn has long had a reputation for remoteness. In 1899, an article in the *Northern Weekly Gazette* noted that 'eleven consecutive weeks have sometimes passed without as much as a shadow of a stranger crossing the threshold', and that 'during the summer months an eighteen-gallon cask of ale lasts a whole month, and in winter three'. Thanks to the motor vehicle many more people visit the inn now. However, it doesn't pay to be complacent. The surrounding moorland is wild, and in winter snow can quickly close the access road. Many an unlucky (or lucky?) visitor has been forced to hunker down at Tan Hill when wintry weather closed in unexpectedly. Sometimes, however, people deliberately make their way to Tan Hill Inn when heavy snow is forecast.

In January 2025, Robyn Vinter, a roving correspondent for *The Guardian*, did just that. In the company of photographer Gary Calton, she arrived at the inn just before the road closed. It was, she wrote, 'a story I've been hoping to cover for years'. Ultimately, Robyn and Gary spent three days at Tan Hill with roughly 30 other customers and staff, unable to leave but enjoying every minute of it. Fortunately for the group, the inn has its own generator and 'enough food for about a month'. During the enforced stay, people drank, ate good food, made new friends and had snowball fights. As a bonus, Agatha the dog, owned by fellow 'inmate' Kip, celebrated her birthday at the inn with a bowl of sausages.

ADDRESS Tan Hill, Reeth, North Yorkshire, DL11 6ED, +44 (0)1833 533007, www.tanhillinn.com TIP Otley has more pubs per head than any other town or village in the Yorkshire Dales.

73 Thwaite

What's in a name?

The Vikings have something of a bad reputation. Mostly, it has to be said, for good reason. But, if you look beyond the murdering and pillaging, they did leave a positive mark on Britain. This is very easily seen when you look at a map of the Yorkshire Dales. Scandinavians found a home here sometime in the late eighth century and stayed put. They gave names to the hamlets and villages they founded, names that, with some smudging and blurring from the passing of time, still retain their Old Norse flavour.

Take the charming hamlet of Thwaite in Swaledale, for example. Thwaite in Old Norse was '*thveit*' meaning a space (or meadow) within a forest, cleared for cultivation. Thwaite is often seen as a suffix in place names too, such as Langthwaite in Arkengarthdale. By sticking 'lang' at the start of the name, the settlers wanted you to know that this was a long meadow. Unsurprisingly, Arkengarthdale was also named by Scandinavian settlers and can be translated as the 'valley of Arkill's enclosure'. Who Arkill was is now unknown, but he was probably a local 10th- or 11th-century chieftain. Garth, which is a paddock or yard, is also a common placename component – Aysgarth in Wensleydale being a good example.

Not far east from Thwaite is the village of Muker. The unusual name is also Norse in origin, from '*mjór-akr*' or 'the narrow cultivated field'. A few miles north of Thwaite is Keld, which is derived from the Norse '*kelda*', meaning a 'spring'. Take a walk along the Swale from Keld and you'll soon come to Kisdon Force. Force is a word used in Yorkshire (as well as parts of Cumbria and Scotland) for waterfall, from the Old Norse for waterfall: '*fors*' or '*foss*' (Janet's Foss in Malhamdale has retained this original spelling). And – of course! – there's the word 'swale', after which both the river and the dale are named. This means a low, hollow place and probably finds its origin in '*svalr*', the Old Norse word for cool.

ADDRESS Thwaite, Richmond, North Yorkshire, DL11 6DR, www.yorkshiredales.org.uk **TIP** Have a cosy drink or a bite to eat at Keartons Guest House; you may even find yourself wanting to stay the night.

74 AA telephone box

Immobile phone

Badly behaved drivers who deliberately break the speed limit have been around since the early days of the motor vehicle. In response, the police have long been tasked with trying to catch perpetrators in the act. Modern forces use a variety of tools to achieve this end, including high-tech radar guns or automatic speed cameras. Early traffic police were less well equipped, however, and used simple speed traps to catch drivers flouting the law.

In 1905, to counter such unsporting behaviour, a merry band of Edwardian petrolheads created the Motorists' Mutual Association. The group employed cyclists who moved around an area and, by using signals and salutes, alerted drivers to nearby police activity. Even shortened to MMA, the name was a mouthful and so it was soon shortened to the far pithier Automobile Association (or AA). In the century since, the AA has served the British public by providing roadside assistance when needed, insurance, travel guides and so many other things relating to car and motorcycle ownership. (Other motoring organisations are, of course, available.)

In 1911, the AA began to build sentry boxes for the company's patrol men, inside of which was a phone with a direct line to HQ. From the 1920s onwards, AA members were given keys to these boxes so that help or advice could be requested. In total, 862 of these distinctive black and yellow boxes were built across the country, with the last constructed in 1962.

Technology moves on, however. The AA boxes were gradually pulled down as they became surplus to requirements, a trend that was accelerated when the mobile phone came along. There are now only 19 AA boxes in the entire country, of which Aysgarth 442 is one. Happily, the future of this particular box is secure. Although now *sans* telephone, it has been listed and is looked after by local volunteers who keep it spick and span.

ADDRESS Temple Bank, near Aysgarth, North Yorkshire, DL8 4UL, gobbles.cured.tour TIP Cauldron Falls in the village of West Burton is a picturesque waterfall on Walden Beck that was painted by J. M. W. Turner.

75 Askrigg

The original TV Darrowby

In July 1940, Alf Wight was a newly qualified vet who had just accepted a position in a veterinary practice in Thirsk, a small market town on the edge of the North York Moors. Alf had always wanted to work in the countryside so this appointment suited him admirably. Donald Sinclair, the owner of the practice, had recently joined the RAF and was about to leave for basic training. Alf was tasked with running things until Donald's return to civilian life. This was the start of a career that eventually led to literary immortality.

In 1969, Alf wrote *If Only They Could Talk*, a humorous and fictionalised account of his early years as a vet. At the time, the Royal College of Veterinary Surgeons banned vets from advertising their services. To avoid any potential problems, Alf chose 'James Herriot' as his pen name when the book was published the following year. A sequel, *It Shouldn't Happen to a Vet*, followed in 1972.

Strangely, neither book was a sales success until they were compiled into one volume for the US market. Under the title of *All Creatures Great and Small* (the second line of the hymn 'All Things Bright and Beautiful'), the book was a smash hit and stayed on *The New York Times* Best Seller list for eight months.

All Creatures Great and Small was a success for the BBC too. In 1978, the corporation adapted the book for television and it instantly proved popular. The series was largely filmed in the Dales, with the village of Askrigg standing in for the fictional town of Darrowby. Fans of the series will instantly recognise Skeldale House on the corner of Market Place, where Herriot lived and worked with fellow vets, Siegfried Farnon and his brother Tristan (the former based on Donald Sinclair). Further up the road is the King's Arms Hotel, renamed The Drovers Arms in the series. And opposite is St Oswald's, the church in which Herriot married his sweetheart, Helen Alderson, in the penultimate episode of series one.

ADDRESS Askrigg, North Yorkshire, DL8 3HT, www.yorkshiredales.org.uk **TIP** A section of the original BBC Skeldale House surgery set is on display in Richmondshire Museum (www.richmondshiremuseum.org.uk).

76 Aysgarth Falls

Movie Star

Robin Hood may have been a hero to the poor and dispossessed but he was no navigator. In the 1991 movie *Robin Hood: Prince of Thieves*, Robin of Locksley (Kevin Costner), having fought in the Crusades, lands back in England near the Seven Sisters, a series of chalk cliffs found in East Sussex. In the company of Azeem (Morgan Freeman), Robin travels north to his home in Nottinghamshire. However, he first stops off at Hadrian's Wall in Northumberland, 200 miles further north. He then makes his way south again only to be temporarily delayed when trying to cross the river Ure at Aysgarth Falls (Upper Force). 'In my dreams alone have I imagined such a place', exclaims Azeem appreciatively.

However, life is never that simple for Robin. A fight kicks off when Will Scarlett (Christian Slater) and his fugitive friends emerge from the surrounding woodland to taunt our hero and demand a toll. Robin is pitted against John Little (Nick Brimble) and the two fight on the falls. Although John is larger and stronger, Robin uses his Nottinghamshire noggin and bests his opponent, whom he renames Little John. Happily, the two make up and Robin joins the outlaws in their fight against the truly wicked (but wonderfully charismatic) Sheriff of Nottingham (Alan Rickman).

It's not hard to see why Kevin Reynolds, the movie's director, picked Aysgarth Falls as a suitable location for the scene. It is a very photogenic place, with the river wide and relatively shallow here. Upper Force is one of three waterfalls found along this stretch of the river: Middle and Lower Force are just a short walk away and, although equally beautiful, are less accessible to visitors and passing medieval heroes. The falls were also featured in *Emily Brontë's Wuthering Heights*, released in 1992. This movie was actually set in Yorkshire and so Heathcliff (Ralph Fiennes) and Cathy (Juliette Binoche) were at least roughly in the right place.

ADDRESS Church Bank, Aysgarth, North Yorkshire, DL8 3TH, +44 (0)1969 662910, www.yorkshiredales.org.uk TIP Take a walk to the summit of Addlebrough and visit the Devil's Stone, a huge glacial erratic boulder (blanking.accusing.directly).

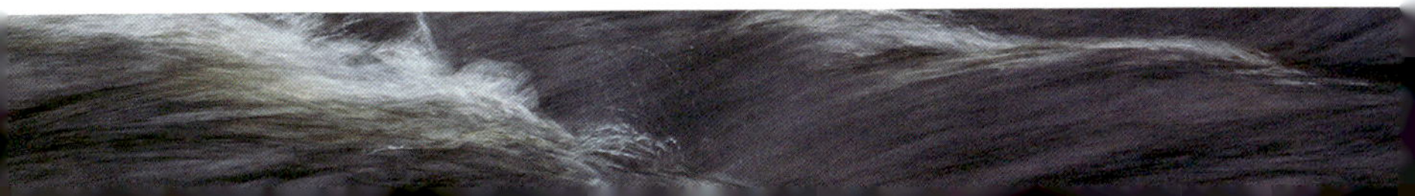

77 Bellerby Ranges

You can't come in...

There is much to see and do in the Yorkshire Dales. However, there are some areas that are *definitely* off limits. Bellerby Ranges north of Leyburn is one of those places. The ranges are one small part of the extensive Catterick Training Area and are used by the British Army for live-fire rifle firing and tactical training. When red flags are displayed (red lamps when it's dark) don't be surprised if you hear the staccato rattle of gunfire as you pass.

The training area serves Catterick Garrison, a military town south of Richmond. The town has a population of 14,000, making it a sizeable community indeed. Remarkably, however, Catterick Garrison did not exist until the 20th century.

The year 1907 was a significant one for Robert Baden-Powell. In August of that year he took a group of boys to Brownsea Island for a week of camping. Baden-Powell was a British hero who had successfully defended Mafeking for eight months during the Boer War. Brownsea Island was designed to test ideas for his forthcoming book *Scouting for Boys*. The camp was a success and led to the formation of the Boy Scout movement the following year. In October 1907, Baden-Powell was appointed to command the Northumbrian Division of the newly formed Territorial Force (the name changed later to the Territorial Army).

Baden-Powell was initially headquartered at Richmond Castle. This, however, proved too small and so land was acquired in the parish of Hipswell to establish a camp for 40,000 men. The camp was originally meant to be temporary, and was even relegated to housing German prisoners at the end of World War I. A permanent garrison was deemed necessary in 1921 when the British lost the use of the Curragh in County Kildare after Irish independence. Since then Catterick has grown and gradually morphed into what is now the largest British Army garrison in the world.

ADDRESS Whipperdale Bank, Leyburn, North Yorkshire, DL8 5JX, www.gov.uk, atoms.linguists.themes TIP Learn more about a renowned Yorkshire army regiment at the Green Howards Museum in Richmond (www.greenhowards.org.uk).

78 Bolton Castle

(Temporary) home of a Scottish queen

Richard le Scrope wanted a place he could truly call his own and he wanted it built in the heart of the Yorkshire Dales. As he was from Norman nobility, and was knighted for his services to Richard II after the Battle of Neville's Cross, le Scrope also wanted to make a statement. And so in 1378, he commissioned a castle that, as it was near the village of Bolton in Wensleydale, has been known as Bolton Castle ever since. After 18 years of hard work, and at a cost of £12,000, le Scrope's stronghold was complete.

The castle still exudes an air of purpose and power today. Strangely, this is something of an illusion. Unlike other similar structures of the period, Bolton Castle was never graced with a moat or even a defensive outer ditch, and there is no inner portcullis. It seems that le Scrope did not feel the need to build an impregnable fortress. Instead, he created a home for himself and his family, albeit a home with outer walls six feet thick. To achieve domestic bliss, le Scrope had his architect, John Lewyn, add plenty of fireplaces to keep everyone warm, as well as provide a decent number of garderobes, the medieval name for a privy.

Bolton Castle's unusually comfortable (for the period) living spaces made it the ideal place for Elizabeth I to park her troublesome cousin, Mary, Queen of Scots, after the latter's defeat at the Battle of Langside in 1568. Mary spent six months imprisoned in Bolton Castle under the watchful eye of Sir Francis Knollys, an English courtier. The Scottish queen was treated well, however. She lived in her own apartments in the south-west tower along with 30 servants and ladies-in-waiting. Mary was raised in France and so spoke French, Latin and Lowland Scots, and it was at Bolton Castle that she first learnt to speak English. To make her brief stay more pleasant her rooms were decorated with rugs and tapestries borrowed from houses nearby.

ADDRESS Castle Bolton, North Yorkshire, DL8 4ET, +44 (0)1969 623981, www.boltoncastle.co.uk **TIP** Go for a trip on the Wensleydale Railway, a heritage line that opened in 2003. The railway terminates at Leyburn, just a short drive from Bolton Castle (www.wensleydale-railway.co.uk).

79 Dales Countryside Museum

How it once was

If Marie Hartley and Ella Pontefract had never met then many original artefacts that tell the story of the Yorkshire Dales would now be lost. In April 1940, 'local worthy' Mr Ralph Horne, died aged 76. Horne was a jeweller and antiques dealer in Leyburn who also ran a popular private museum. The museum boasted an eclectic set of objects, many of which were connected to the Dales. The following year the contents of the museum were put up for auction by Horne's son. Fearing that this would result in the collection being scattered, Marie and Ella bought 13 lots. This far-sighted act laid the foundation of what is now the Dales Countryside Museum.

Marie and Ella continued to add to their collection. When word about their acquisitions spread, locals began to donate goods and items of interest. Sadly, Ella died in 1945 at the all-too-young age of 48. After Ella's death, Marie was assisted by Joan Ingilby, who had expert knowledge of the social history of the Yorkshire Dales. Joan also provided the invaluable service of documenting objects in a card index as they were acquired.

By the end of the 1960s, Marie and Joan had effectively created a museum (larger exhibits were kept in a cart shed, and the smaller pieces in a house the pair rented in Askrigg). Realising that the collection required more space, Marie and Joan offered it to what was then the North Riding County Council in 1972. Eventually, after the collection had been in storage for nine years, the Upper Dales Folk Museum was opened in what was once a railway goods warehouse. Since 1990, the renamed Dales Countryside Museum has been run by the Yorkshire Dales National Park Authority.

The museum is exactly how all museums should be. It is so jam-packed with interesting and wonderful things from the region that one visit won't be enough.

ADDRESS Station Yard, Burtersett Road, Hawes, North Yorkshire, DL8 3NT, +44 (0)1969 666210, www.dalescountrysidemuseum.org.uk **TIP** See local farmer Richard Fawcett give sheepdog demonstrations during the summer and autumn months (www.sheepdogdemo.co.uk).

80 Edwardian Rock Garden

One man's vision

In 1998, Angela and Peter Jauneika, along with their two children, made the sensible decision to move north from Staffordshire to the heart of the Yorkshire Dales. The family's new home was Heather Cottage in the picturesque village of Aysgarth. What the Jauneikas hadn't given much thought to was a small parcel of rocky and overgrown land that came with the property. They soon discovered that they'd acquired a historically important garden created by a very wealthy and more-than-slightly eccentric individual.

What is now known as the Edwardian Rock Garden was originally created by Frank Sayer-Graham. Sayer-Graham was born in 1859 and had made his fortune farming silver rabbits and selling their fur to traders in Russia. However, his real calling in life was gardening. In 1906, he commissioned Backhouse Nurseries of York to create an alpine rock garden opposite Heather Cottage, his childhood home. The work was overseen by W. A. Clark, who was a highly experienced gardener; he had previously created a 30-foot replica of the Matterhorn in the garden of Sir Frank Crisp at Henley-on-Thames. The limestone to create Sayer-Graham's garden came from local moors (an act that is now thoroughly illegal), and the plants from Backhouse, many of which were illustrated in Clark's book, *Alpine Plants*, published in 1901.

Sayer-Graham lovingly tended to his garden until his death in 1946. The garden then passed through the hands of several owners and slowly began to deteriorate. A proposal to flatten the garden in 1988 was met with horror by locals. Fortunately, the fuss led to the garden being granted Grade II listing by English Heritage.

Angela Jauneika was determined to restore the garden to its former glory. After raising funds, 80 per cent of which came from the Heritage Lottery Fund, Angela set to work. In 2002, the newly completed garden was opened to the public.

ADDRESS Constable House, Thornton Road, Leyburn, North Yorkshire, DL8 3AJ, lorry.cushy.before **TIP** St Andrew's Church in Aysgarth boasts a wonderful, colourful rood screen created in the early 16th century and originally installed in Jervaulx Abbey.

81 Hardraw Force

The long drop

If you find yourself at a loose end then try working out how many waterfalls there are in the Yorkshire Dales. This is a task guaranteed to keep you occupied for a *very* good while. Arguably, Hardraw Force should be number one on your list, for it is thought to be England's highest unbroken waterfall. It is a very popular tourist attraction whatever the weather or season for this reason. And so, over the years, it has seen some very distinguished visitors. The artist J. M. W. Turner was one of these. The pencil sketches he made on the day were later used to create etchings and watercolours.

Hardraw Force also featured in the movie *Robin Hood: Prince of Thieves*, released in 1991. After a hard day's outlawing, Robin (Kevin Costner) has a refreshing bath in the pool below the waterfall. What he doesn't realise is that, from a high vantage point, Marian (Mary Elizabeth Mastrantonio) is keenly studying his ablutions. And his bare bottom. The sight obviously stirs something less than innocent in the maiden's heart for the pair are wed at the movie's end. Or perhaps it's Robin's sheer pluck and unfailing nobility that do the trick. You decide.

The poet William Wordsworth, in the company of his sister, Dorothy, visited the waterfall in the winter of 1799. Afterwards, in a letter to fellow poet Samuel Taylor Coleridge, he described how the cliff face was 'like a wall extending itself over our heads, like the ceiling of a huge cave, from the summit of which the waters shot directly over our heads into a basin'.

A Dr P. Hinkes Bird paid a visit to the waterfall in 1878 and felt compelled to write an article for the *Lytham and Kirkham Times* about his experience. The good doctor, no poet alas, was more inclined to be scientific in his appraisal: 'the stream of water has a clear fall of 99 feet into a natural amphitheatre, the walls of which are perhaps 200 feet high, and perfectly perpendicular'.

ADDRESS Hardraw, Leyburn, North Yorkshire, DL8 3LZ, +44 (0)1969 667572, www.hardrawforce.com **TIP** The Green Dragon Inn is a splendid traditional pub where you can buy a pint or sit down to a hearty meal (www.thegreendragonhardraw.co.uk).

82 Holy Trinity Church

Layers of history

Like many English churches, Holy Trinity Church in the village of Wensley has been altered many times since its original foundation. The oldest parts of the church date back to the mid 13th century. The southern wall of the chancel is one such part and features three single lancet windows. The northern chancel wall, however, dates from the 15th century, when a vestry and a lodging for the priest were also added. The tower was rebuilt in the 18th century, and the box pews added early in the 19th. And the roof was repaired and whitewash was removed from the interior walls of the church in 1927. Wonderfully, the latter improvement revealed medieval paintings depicting Biblical twin brothers Jacob and Esau.

Perhaps the most striking aspect of the church is the carved woodwork, which dates from the early 16th century. The pew ends, for instance, feature a variety of fantastical beasts, as well as floral designs and the coats of arms of local worthies.

Another notable wooden structure inside the church is the Scrope chantry screen. The Scrope (pronounced 'Scroop') family were of Norman stock and owned large areas of land in northern England. Nearby Bolton Castle was commissioned by the first prominent Scrope, Richard le Scrope. The chantry screen was originally made for Easby Abbey, but was moved to Holy Trinity after the dissolution of Easby in the 16th century.

However, there are elements of the screen that are not original. Many of the heraldic elements on the screen were 'revived' by architect George Shaw in the mid 19th century. Shaw specialised in building as well as renovating churches in the Gothic style popular at the time; Holy Trinity was just one of many that benefitted from Shaw's sympathetic restoration during his relatively short life. Shaw was also a forger who sneakily sold well-crafted but utterly fake Tudor and Jacobean furniture to the aristocracy.

ADDRESS Low Lane, Wensley, North Yorkshire, DL8 4HX, www.visitchurches.org.uk
TIP Curlew Dairy is a small micro dairy based in Wensley that produces traditional hand-made Wensleydale and Yoredale cheese (www.curlewdairy.co.uk).

83 Jervaulx Abbey

A Tudor king makes a few changes...

Henry VIII, king of England and Wales from 1509 to 1547, has a lot to answer for. One far-reaching consequence of his reign came about when he decided to annul his marriage to his first wife, Catherine of Aragon. A vivacious young woman named Anne Boleyn had caught his eye and he really wanted to be married to her instead. Unfortunately for Henry, he needed the blessing of Pope Clement VII, who did not play ball. And so the impatient king came up with a terrific wheeze: circumvent the pope and name himself (who else?) as the Supreme Head of the Church of England.

Breaking with Papal authority also allowed Henry to seize and sell off the assets of the country's many monasteries, starting in 1536. This helped swell the king's coffers very nicely indeed (which he largely spent on military adventures). Unhappily, it also resulted in the destruction of fine abbeys and monasteries, many of which had provided valuable services in their local communities.

One such establishment was Jervaulx Abbey. Jervaulx was built in 1155 and was run by the Order of Cistercians, who were known as the white monks due to the colour of their cowls. The curiously Gallic name derives from the French for 'the Ure valley' and is not dissimilar to Yoredale, an alternative name for Wensleydale.

Jervaulx Abbey has had a good number of owners since the 16th century. The first was Matthew Stuart, fourth Earl of Lennox, who was granted the site by Henry. Jervaulx Abbey is currently owned by the Burdon family, who purchased the property in 1971. The latest custodian is Ian Burdon, who now runs the estate and looks after what remains of the abbey buildings. Collectively, the Burdon family has done much in the past 50 or so years to protect and conserve the abbey for the future. Supported by English Heritage, the ruins have been extensively and carefully consolidated and strengthened, ready to face the next five centuries.

ADDRESS Jervaulx, East Witton, Ripon, North Yorkshire, HG4 4PH, +44 (0)1677 460391, www.jervaulxabbey.com TIP On a warm day why not cool down with an ice cream at Brymor. The ice cream is hand made using local milk and comes in a wide range of tempting flavours (www.brymordairy.co.uk).

84 Middleham Castle

Childhood home of a king

There's a period of English history that's a bit of a slog if you want to memorise who was king at the time. For over 400 years, from the 12th century onwards, there is an endless procession of Edwards, Richards and Henrys, with only the occasional Stephen or John to vary things. Some of these kings were good, some were mediocre and one or two were absolute stinkers. Richard III reigned during this span of time and his reputation is… complicated.

Richard was born in 1452 in Northamptonshire, but was raised in Middleham Castle in Wensleydale. He was the 11th child of Richard, third Duke of York and Cecily Neville. As a direct descendant of Edward III, the elder Richard felt that he had a strong claim to the English throne. Unfortunately, members of the House of Lancaster disagreed. This difference of opinion led to bloody civil war, better known to us as the War of the Roses.

The junior Richard became king in 1483 after the death of his elder brother, Edward IV, who had reigned as king for 22 years, and Edward's 12-year-old son (another Edward), who only managed to reign for three months for reasons that we'll return to. Richard didn't last long as king either. Henry Tudor wanted the throne and he had an army to help him take it. The two men and their supporters met in battle at Bosworth Field on 22 August, 1485. Although Richard had a larger army it was Henry who prevailed. Richard was killed and his army defeated. Henry VII was crowned king a few months later and reigned for 24 years.

Tudor propaganda cast Richard as a villain and for that reason he is generally seen as one of the stinkers. One particularly vicious rumour spread by the victors was that he'd had his young nephews Edward V (hence the short reign) and (yet another!) Richard imprisoned in the Tower of London and then murdered. This may – or may not – be true, though no one now knows for certain.

ADDRESS Castle Hill, Middleham, North Yorkshire, DL8 4QG, +44 (0)370 3331181, www.english-heritage.org.uk **TIP** Look for the market cross at the centre of the village. It dates back to the medieval period.

85 Penhill Preceptory

Medieval burial site

The Poor Fellow-Soldiers of Christ and of the Temple of Solomon, fortunately more widely known as the Knights Templar, was a Catholic military order founded in 1118. They were involved in the church's prosecution of the Crusades, either protecting Christian pilgrims in Jerusalem or taking part in the actual fighting. They also created what were essentially early banks, giving the order enormous financial influence. However, the order collapsed in the early 14th century when Philip IV of France, who was jealous of the Templars' power, began to persecute its members. In 1312, Pope Clement V officially disbanded the order. And that was that.

In 1840, a Mr W. J. Anderson, then of Swinithwaite Hall, discovered ruins on the slopes of Penhill. This turned out to be a part of a Knights Templar preceptory. According to a reporter for the *Leeds Mercury*, Anderson ('a gentleman of refined taste') found 'stone coffins opened out containing the bones of the warrior-monks', as well as 'armour, bits and spurs and other articles'.

A preceptory is a small (often rural) monastery built by orders such as the Knights Templar, often to raise money for their military activities. The Penhill Preceptory, built in 1142, owes its existence to Norman knight Roger de Mowbray. De Mowbray was a supporter of the Knights Templar and funded the construction of the preceptory, supplying both land and timber. He also fought in a number of crusades, the last when he was in his sixties.

Penhill Preceptory was dedicated to Our Lady and St Catherine. All that can be seen now are the scant remains of the preceptory's chapel. Inside the low walls you can still see some of the open graves described in the *Leeds Mercury* (the bones are long gone). The fate of Penhill Preceptory mirrored that of the Knights Templar. In 1338, by which date the estate was owned by Geoffrey le Scrope, the preceptory buildings were in ruins.

ADDRESS Swinithwaite, North Yorkshire, DL8 4UJ, www.historicengland.org.uk, goodbyes.releases.knee **TIP** If you're in the mood for some lunchtime fish and chips then visit the Wensleydale Heifer and choose from their extensive Heifer Lunchtime Chippie menu (www.wensleydaleheifer.co.uk).

86 Sorrelsykes Follies

Fly me to the moon

Architecture doesn't have to be particularly old to be enigmatic. On a ridge overlooking Sorrelsykes House are three stone structures, the origins of which are surprisingly shrouded in mystery. Known locally as the Sorrelsykes Follies, they were built sometime in the mid or possibly the late 19th century (when the house had the less appealing name of Sorrowsikes).

The follies are unusually abstract in shape. The largest and most striking is referred to as the 'Rocket Ship' thanks to its streamlined conical shape sitting on what looks like a square launch pad supported by sturdy buttresses. On one side of the 'launchpad' is a doorway leading to an interior space. Above the doorway is an oculus, a round window the word for which is derived from the Latin for eye. The second folly is known as the 'Pepper Pot' and did find use at one point in its history as a place to cure bacon (like the 'Rocket Ship', the 'Pepper Pot' also has a doorway leading inside). The smallest folly is perhaps the strangest of all. It is a simple square arch but one that is too small to walk under. More gruesome writers have noted that it somewhat resembles a guillotine (if you squint). There was once a fourth folly higher up the hill too. This was a more 'traditional' folly and was built in the form of a fake castle façade. Sadly this was destroyed during a storm in the early 1990s.

The follies may (or may not) have been commissioned by one or all of the four daughters of Edward Tennant: Isabella, Rebecca, Emma and Ann. The family had the means to create such frivolous structures. Rebecca, for instance, was a shareholder in the Swaledale and Wensleydale Banking Company. In an 1852 directory of joint-stock and private banks in England her profession is listed as 'gentlewoman'. They may have been built purely for the amusement of the sisters, as a project for apprentice stonemasons, or possibly to help out local workers during an economic downturn.

ADDRESS Sorrelsykes, North Yorkshire, DL8 4UW, slate.gravest.purifier, copycat.megawatt.script and commuting.movie.cheered TIP West Burton has a wonderfully large village square that boasts a playground, war memorial and The Old Smithy Antiques shop (www.yorkshiredales.org.uk).

87 Wensley

Overlooked

What determines the name of a dale? A good proportion are named after the river that flows through the dale, such as Swaledale, Ribblesdale and Coverdale (a dale is just the local name for a river valley, after all). The origins of some names are more obscure. The 'gar' in Garsdale was possibly a person or perhaps a prominent geographic feature but no one can now say for certain which it is. And then there are those Dales logically named after the most important village or town in the area, such as Dentdale and Malhamdale. Wensleydale is one of these dales. Strangely however, the village of Wensley is really rather unassuming and far, far smaller than the neighbouring towns of Leyburn or Hawes, just a few miles to the east and west respectively.

So why isn't the dale known as Leyburndale or Hawesdale? Or even, for that matter, Uredale, after the river Ure? Oddly enough, the dale was known by some as Uredale in the past. Sort of. Edmund Bogg preferred Yoredale and referred to the dale as such in his 1925 book *Beautiful Wensleydale and By the Banks of Yore* (his spelling of Ure). Though you do have to ignore the slightly contradictory use of 'Wensleydale' in the book's title.

Though it's hard to imagine it now, Wensley *was* once the most important village in the dale. In 1202, Hugh Malebiche gave King John a palfrey (a horse bred for riding) for the right to hold a market in Wensley on a Thursday. For almost a century this was the only market in the dale and so Wensley thrived to become the dominant regional economic power.

Wensley's time in the sun ended in 1563 when plague arrived in the village. Many died and the survivors fled to the nearby Leyburn. After this, Leyburn rose to ascendancy and Wensley withered, eventually losing its weekly market. But by then the village had given its name to Wensleydale, so arguably had a victory of sorts.

ADDRESS A684, DL8 4HJ, North Yorkshire, www.yorkshiredales.org.uk
TIP See how traditional candles are made at White Rose Candles in Wensley (www.whiterosecandles.com).

88 Dibble's Bridge

The Devil lends a hand

The Barden Triangle may not be as famous as its three-sided twin in the Bermudas, but it is arguably more mysterious. It is an area in Lower Wharfedale that includes such spooky and supernatural locations as Troller's Gill, Elbolton Hill (the 'Hill of the Fairies'), and Dibble's Bridge, the subject of this chapter.

The stone bridge that carries the B6265 over the river Dibb is a handsome if commonplace structure. According to legend an older bridge on the site was built for a local shoemaker named Ralph Calvert by… the Devil. Twice a year Calvert had to make the long journey to pay rent due to the Abbot of Fountain's Abbey, as well as return shoes he had repaired for the monks. During the night before one such trek, Calvert had a wild and frightening dream about the Devil. He dreamt that the fiend accosted him in the ravine where he usually forded the Dibb. There the Devil tried to force Calvert into a large sack, no doubt intending to drag the poor shoemaker to hell. Or possibly Lancashire.

Still haunted by his vivid dream, Calvert set out the following morning. At first all went well. He arrived safely at the abbey, paid his rent and delivered the newly repaired shoes. On his return, however, Calvert discovered that the Dibb was a raging torrent. Fearing for his life, he carefully waded and swam across the swollen river. Safely reaching the other side, Calvert sat down to rest and recover. Thinking that he was alone, he began to sing a song to himself. He was therefore disconcerted when another voice joined in. At this, Calvert's blood ran cold. Was his dream about to come true? Horror of horrors, it *was* the Devil but, having shared a song with Calvert, Old Nick was in an obliging mood. The Devil asked Calvert what he would like most. Calvert asked that a bridge be constructed across the ravine to make his twice-yearly journey easier. This the Devil was happy to do, much to Calvert's delight.

ADDRESS On the B6265, Skipton, North Yorkshire, BD23 5EE, escalated.unionists.jazzy TIP The Craven Arms Pub in nearby Appletreewick (pronounced 'app-trick') is famous for its annual ferret race, held every February (www.craven-cruckbarn.co.uk).

89 Fleet Moss

Quilty pleasure

Blanket bog or blanket mire is a flat, wet expanse of peatland formed by high levels of rainfall and poor drainage. It is a bleak, treeless and often seemingly featureless landscape. Very few plants can thrive in the nutrient-poor and acidic conditions found in blanket bog. As a result, cottongrass and heather predominate, as well as mosses and specialist species such as sundew. Unsurprisingly, wading birds find a happy home in blanket bog, such as curlew and dunlin, as well as species such as short-eared owl.

This may not sound all that appealing – it's not a place you'd want to spend *all* your precious holiday time, perhaps. But, although blanket bog may not have the colourful charisma of heather moorland or the lofty splendour of upland fell, it should be celebrated nevertheless. There is approximately 2.25 million hectares of blanket bog in the United Kingdom, mainly in Scotland. In the Yorkshire Dales, Fleet Moss, nestled neatly between Wharfedale and Wensleydale, contributes 102 hectares to this total.

Most people experience Fleet Moss… fleetingly. A road passes through the area, connecting the villages of Oughtershaw and Gayle to one another. Reaching a height of 1,975 feet, the road has the distinction of being the highest paved road in Yorkshire. In places it has a gradient of 20 per cent. Despite – or perhaps even because of – this, the route is popular with cyclists.

Areas of blanket bog such as Fleet Moss are carbon sinks – it's been estimated that the UK's blanket bogs store 3.2 *billion* tonnes of carbon. They also help to prevent flooding elsewhere and have a cooling effect on the climate too. Unfortunately, Fleet Moss has suffered badly from erosion. This has resulted in the creation of huge lifeless channels that will take decades to repair. So badly scarred is Fleet Moss that it has been nicknamed 'The Somme'. A restoration project is now underway to repair the damage.

ADDRESS Oughtershaw Road, North Yorkshire, DL8 3DQ, www.yorkshiredales.org.uk, tadpoles.remain.committed **TIP** West of Fleet Moss is Dodd Fell Hill, the 24th highest hill in the Yorkshire Dales (rocker.bucket.twinkled).

90 Grassington

The new TV Darrowby

Grassington is a bustling modern town where you can easily find many 21st-century amenities, such as EV charging stations and cafés with Wi-Fi. In recent years, however, the town has often found itself transported back to the 1940s, a decade when petrol was rationed and telephones had rotary dials. To add to the confusion, the town is then referred to as Darrowby.

Fans of *All Creatures Great and Small* will of course know that Darrowby is the fictional village invented by Alf Wight for his best-selling series of books about life as a rural vet. In 2020, Grassington was chosen by Playground Entertainment as the ideal place to recreate the village for a small-screen reboot of *All Creatures*, made for and broadcast by Channel 5.

Channel 5 set itself a difficult task when it decided to commission the show. *All Creatures* was first adapted by the BBC in 1978 and is much loved by many even now. Fortunately, the new version has proved to be a critical and popular success, both in Britain and abroad. In February 2026 it was announced that filming for the seventh series had begun and that an eighth series was a certainty.

A lot of work is involved turning Grassington into Darrowby. Filming is largely restricted to the town's market square, but even within this relatively small area any signs of modernity must be removed or disguised. The Stripey Badger book shop becomes G. F. Endleby, Darrowby's friendly greengrocers, and the exterior of the Devonshire Inn is altered to stand in for The Drovers Arms (the interior scenes are shot at Hardraw's Green Dragon).

Skeldale House, where Herriot (Nicholas Ralph) lives with his wife Helen (Rachel Shenton), and where he works with fellow vets Siegfried (Samuel West) and Tristan Farnon (Callum Woodhouse), is a private residence just off the square that, when filming starts, gains a natty portico to disguise its modern features.

ADDRESS The Square, Grassington, North Yorkshire, CA17 4JT, www.yorkshiredales.co.uk TIP Choose from a wide range of freshly made home-cooked food and hot and cold drinks at the Cobblestones Café (www.cobblestonescafe.co.uk).

91 Hebden Suspension Bridge

Saving lives

In 1884 a man named Joseph Slack attempted to cross the river Wharfe not far from the village of Hebden. The only route to the other side was via a long series of stepping stones. Unluckily for Joseph, a fierce storm further up the valley had created a huge torrent of water that surged swiftly along the river. Unable to get to safety in time, poor Joseph was overwhelmed by the deluge, swept away and drowned.

Something needed to be done and so a committee was formed to discuss the building of a bridge. One committee member was Thomas Francis Hammond, a shopkeeper in Hebden, who, along with his colleagues, decided on a suspension bridge. It was also resolved that it should be built near to the stepping stones.

The Revd Charles Henry Carlisle, another committee member, helped organise a public subscription to help pay for the bridge. In total, over £80 (roughly equivalent to £13,500) was raised this way. With the finance in place, construction of the bridge proceeded apace. On 26 September, 1885, a lavish ceremony was held to officially open Hebden's new and handsome bridge. A marquee was raised on the village's side of the Wharfe and a crowd of some 500 were – on payment of one shilling per person – treated to tea and entertained by a brass band. Since that date, Hebden suspension bridge has provided a safe place for folk to cross the Wharfe and so avoid the watery demise that befell Joseph Slack.

At least that's the official story. Strangely, there is no report of the drowning in any local newspaper archive. And Joseph Slack – who definitely did exist – had met his end in 1869, though there is no record of the cause. Joseph's tragic death became an established 'fact' thanks to the memoirs of Hammond, published in 1927. But, even if the tale is false, the bridge is wonderful.

ADDRESS Near Mill Lane, Hebden, North Yorkshire, BD23 5DY, slung.vocals.darting TIP Go for a cup of tea and slice of home-made cake (or two) in the atmospheric setting of the Old School Tea Room (www.theoldschooltearoom.com).

92 Hubberholme

Poet praises parish

The small (but perfectly formed) village of Hubberholme has very ancient roots. Remains have been found on nearby moorland that provide strong evidence that Bronze and Iron Age people made the area their home. The village's name is thought to have Viking or Anglo-Scandinavian origins – probably deriving from the pleasingly melodious 'Hubba's (or Hūnburg's) homestead'. And, although the earliest part of the church of St Michael and All Angels dates to the 12th century, there was probably an older church on the site built long before the Norman invasion of 1066.

One individual who particularly appreciated Hubberholme was the poet, dramatist, novelist and all-round overachiever, John Boynton (J. B.) Priestley. Priestley was born on 13 September, 1894, in Manningham, an industrial suburb of Bradford in the West Riding of Yorkshire. The poet mentioned Hubberholme in a number of his works, always praising the village's many wonderful qualities. Priestley was so enamoured of Hubberholme that, after his death in 1984, his ashes were buried in a secret location in the churchyard of St Michael and All Angels. A plaque in the church touchingly records that Priestley 'loved the Dales and found Hubberholme "one of the smallest and pleasantest places in the world"'.

Inside St Michael and All Angels you'll find a handsome set of oak pews, choir stalls and chairs, all created by Robert 'Mouseman' Thompson. Like Priestley, Thompson was a Yorkshireman. He acquired his peculiar nickname in 1919 after he (on a whim) carved a mouse onto the cornice of a screen he was working on. The mouse became his signature and every piece of furniture he worked on subsequently featured one. Thompson died aged 79 in 1955 and was buried in Kilburn, Yorkshire. Happily, the studio he founded still thrives to this day. His final instruction to his grandson Robert was to 'remember to keep the timber yard full'.

ADDRESS Hubberholme, North Yorkshire, BD23 5JE, www.yorkshiredales.co.uk TIP The nearby hamlet of Yockenthwaite stands in for the fictional Aldersons' Farm in the Channel 5 version of *All Creatures Great and Small*.

93 Kilnsey Crag

Overhang

Kilnsey Crag is one of Wharfedale's most recognisable landmarks. The huge limestone cliff looms over the village of Kilnsey; if you're making for Kilnsey then you really have no excuse for not being able to find the place. The limestone beds that form the crag were laid down during the Carboniferous period some 330 million years ago. However, the crag's most noteworthy feature – its distinctive overhang – was scooped out by a glacier during the last ice age.

Kilnsey Crag is understandably popular with climbers and there are a good number of routes up the cliff face recorded by UK Climbing (UKC describes Kilnsey as 'One of Yorkshire's "Big Three" limestone crags, the other two being Gordale and Malham'.) As is the way of these things, many of the routes have decidedly whimsical names, such as 'The Diedre', 'Let them eat Jelly Beans' and 'Metal Mickey'. The hardest route on the UKC list is 'Tragedy into the Bulge'. With a grade of 8a+, it is a route that should only be tackled by experienced climbers.

A particular highlight of the annual Kilnsey Show is the Crag Race. The race made its debut at the very first show in 1897 and has been held virtually every year since. Just over a mile in length and with a 400-foot climb, the route is challenging to say the least. Runners first scramble up a steep scree slope, risking ankles (and every other bone in their body) to reach the summit of the crag. The way back down to the show ground is no picnic either. The scariest stretch is arguably the chimney, a 40-foot near-vertical descent down a narrow rocky gully (a rope is thoughtfully attached to one of the rock walls, you'll be pleased to learn). The record for completing the course is a mind-boggling seven minutes and thirty-five seconds and was set by Mick Hawkins in 1982. Almost the entire route is visible from the show ground so non-participants can see all the 'fun' that they're missing out on.

ADDRESS Kilnsey Park, Kilnsey, North Yorkshire, BD23 5PS, +44 (0)1756 752150, www.kilnseypark.co.uk **TIP** See Wharfedale from the back of a pony with Kilnsey Trekking and Riding (www.kilnseyriding.com).

94 Scarecrow Festival

'Well I'll be bum-swizzled!'

Kettlewell is a *very* pleasant place to be at any time of the year. However, if you suffer from formidophobia – a fear of scarecrows – then you may want to give the village a miss during the second week in August. For this is when the Kettlewell Scarecrow Festival is held. And so all that week there is no escaping the things; they are *everywhere* you turn.

The first festival was held in 1994 to raise money for Kettlewell Primary School, which serves children from the village as well as from outlying farms and hamlets in Upper Wharfedale. The fundraising aspect to the festival continues to this day, with the village hall and St Mary's Church now also benefitting. The scarecrows are made by the villagers and all are unique. Many represent the profession of the person who made them, but others are pure flights of fancy. Famous pop stars in scarecrow form rub shoulders with straw-filled fictional characters from children's books. The Loch Ness Monster has also been known to make an appearance, as have many other types of animal both wild and tame.

One man had good reason to remember the very first festival. On leaving a pub in Kettlewell one evening, John Clement saw what he thought was a burglar climbing down a ladder. John – who was on holiday and so not from the village – bravely tried to make a citizen's arrest. After a fruitless attempt to call the miscreant down from his perch, John discovered that he was trying to arrest 'Bertie', one of that year's scarecrows.

There are literally hundreds of scarecrows on display during the festival. There are so many that the official festival trail around the village takes at least an hour and more like two. And word has got round. Thousands of visitors flock to Kettlewell during the festival, many of whom return year after year. It truly is fun for all the family, unless you're also prone to enochlophobia…

ADDRESS Kettlewell, North Yorkshire, BD23 5RD, kettlewellscarecrowfestival.co.uk
TIP The Kilnsey Show has been held at the end of summer since 1897 and is a thoroughly fun mix of livestock competitions, home-baking and handicrafts (www.kilnseyshow.co.uk).

95 Starbotton

Village life

Thirty-seven places in the Yorkshire Dales National Park have been granted conservation area status. The village of Starbotton and its surroundings achieved this distinction in 1969. Starbotton is peaceful, charming and boasts much vernacular architecture dating from the 17th century onwards.

As fans of *The Archers* will confirm, a quiet village isn't necessarily one without incident. A letter written by a Christopher Calvert and printed in the *Leeds Intelligencer* on 24 December, 1829, reported a local scandal. Calvert explained that 'a Sum of Money, together with a Pocket-Book, and a Pair of Small Clothes, was stolen from my Dwelling-House, amounting to £48 10s' (a sum equivalent to £4,000 today). A statement by Calvert's apprentice, John Fletcher, in whom Calvert 'placed the greatest Confidence', led to suspicion falling on two locals: William Bell and William Clark. Calvert had applied for a warrant to have their houses searched but this was ultimately never used. Fletcher confessed to the theft and expressed his 'deep Contrition'. In the letter, Calvert apologised to Bell and Clark that they were originally accused of the crime, the apology witnessed by five other inhabitants of Starbotton.

A more shocking story was printed in the *North-Riding Advertiser* on 19 December, 1857. A 'Mr. Thomas Iveson, butcher and cattle dealer, of Gayle near Hawes', was out riding. Somewhere between Kettlewell and Starbotton, Iveson 'was attacked by a highwayman, by whom he was knocked off his horse'. Iveson, who was 'a strong athletic man', fought with his assailant for a quarter of an hour. The poor man was hurt, suffering a 'cut in two places in the fleshy part of his left arm'. Fortunately, he suffered no loss, 'except for his hat and walking stick, which were subsequently found in an adjoining field'. Like many such crimes at the time, this one was never solved and the would-be thief was never caught.

ADDRESS Starbotton, North Yorkshire, BD23 5HY, www.yorkshiredales.org.uk **TIP** Tor Dike (spans.cactus.router) on the hills east of Starbotton is an earthwork built by the rebel Brigantian Chief Venutius in A.D. 70 as a defence against Roman invasion.

96 Stepping Stones

Walking across the Wharfe

There are many ways to cross the river Wharfe. Arguably, none are as nerve-wracking, however, as using the stepping stones laid across the river at Bolton Abbey. Even watching someone else cross can cause the palms to sweat, particularly if they start to look a bit unsteady on their feet. A report in the *Yorkshire Post* on 21 May, 1921, documented this very phenomenon. 'If you have not seen them lately you should go there again and take part in the sport of watching people cross them', advised one of the paper's journalists in a short article. The writer had learnt that on the previous day, 'one man lost his balance, bending his body double several times before regaining it'. Ultimately all was well and 'it was a great moment for onlookers, and no doubt for the man himself'.

Fortunately, accidents are reasonably rare and the water isn't usually that deep. There is also a wooden footbridge nearby for those who don't feel up to the challenge. The key to a successful crossing is not to think too hard about failure. And not to rush even when there is a queue of people waiting to take their turn.

The Wharfe does have a disconcerting tendency to spate after heavy rain, when it becomes a very real danger to life. A venerable local proverb describes the river thus: 'Wharfe is clear and the Aire lithe: Where the Aire drowns one, Wharfe drowns five'. The crossing is therefore closed when the river is in one of its more tempestuous or unpredictable moods. Occasionally, a storm washes away one or more of the stones leaving an unfortunate gap or two. An accident in 1890 led to calls for a rail to be run parallel to the stones. This was resisted in lieu of a bridge, which was built in 1899.

Bolton Abbey was founded in 1154 by Augustinian monks. The 62 stepping stones were originally placed for the benefit of lay workers making their way to the monastery. The crossing is now used purely for fun, even if that fun is entirely vicarious.

ADDRESS Bolton Abbey, North Yorkshire, BD23 6EX, +44 (0)1756 718000, www.boltonabbey.com, countries.agreeable.forever **TIP** The nearby Cavendish Memorial Fountain (prowess.drill.defensive) is a wonderfully incongruous stone structure erected as a tribute to Lord Frederick Cavendish, who was murdered in Dublin in 1882.

97 Tin Bridge

Spoilers! It's made of wood

Follow the footpath south from the Yorkshire Dales National Park car park in Grassington and you'll soon come to a bridge over the river Wharfe. The structure is known locally as the 'Tin Bridge', which is very odd because it's undeniably made from wood. This bridge is the third replacement for one built in the early 18th century. However, it was the second bridge that earned the nickname that still applies to the current crossing.

The first bridge over the river was built by J & W Birkbeck in 1814 for workers employed at their Linton Mill, south of the river. This bridge was replaced in 1860 by one made from steel panels. As these panels corroded they were repaired with flattened patches of tin cut out from drums used in the mill. And it was then that the metallic epithet was first applied. Skipton Rural Council eventually took on responsibility for the bridge. Perhaps horrified at its ramshackle appearance, the council replaced the 'Tin Bridge' with a steel lattice girder bridge in 1904. The modern (and thoroughly wooden) bridge opened in 1989.

Look down from the bridge and you'll see Linton Falls. These can be thunderously spectacular after heavy rain, and are often traversed by canoeists looking for a challenge. The falls were created by a discontinuity formed millions of years ago in the limestone bed of the river Wharfe. Close by the falls are the weirs built to channel water for use by the (now demolished) mill.

Look west and in the distance you'll see Linton Falls Hydro. The first scheme to generate electricity on the Wharfe opened in 1909. The plant was housed in a functional but handsome brick building, next to an existing nine-foot-high weir on the river. The Hydro supplied electricity locally until 1948, when the National Grid made the plant redundant. It was restored and re-opened in 2012, and now generates 500,000 kilowatt hours of electricity annually.

ADDRESS Linton, North Yorkshire, BD23 6BQ, www.yorkshiredales.org.uk, situation.mocked.unloaded **TIP** St Michael's Church in Linton is an interesting mix of original 12th-century architecture and an extensive 19th-century restoration by John Varley of Skipton.

98 Troller's Gill

Beware the Barghest

Demonic black dogs apparently roam the British Isles with truly horrifying abandon. Black Shuck bedevils East Anglia, lurking in the shadows and scaring witless those who meet him. (Is it the wind you hear or is it his unearthly howling? Better run just in case…) North Wales suffers under the rule of Gwyllgi, the Dog of Darkness, a red-eyed wolf-like creature. And the Isle of Man, despite being an island, has somehow acquired the Moddey Dhoo, a phantom dog with 'eyes like coals of fire'.

You may (or may not!) be pleased to learn that northern England and southern Scotland have their own variety of black dog, known as the Barghest. One haunts the West Riding area at night, dragging chains behind him and peering in through the windows of his victims. And, if you're unlucky, you may come across the Barghest who lives in Troller's Gill, a rocky gorge at the heart of Wharfedale. Meeting the Barghest is bad news. It's said that anyone who sees the hound will die within a few days of the encounter. Keeping your eyes shut is no defence, however, as a bite from the Barghest inflicts a wound that never heals. It's also said that when the Barghest howls all the (non-demonic) dogs nearby join in.

How the Barghest got his name is something of a mystery. According to the Reverend William Carr in his comprehensive book *The Dialect of Craven*, published in 1828, a Barghest (or Bar-Guest) is 'a sprite that haunts towns and populous places'; the word derived from 'berg' or place and geest, a ghost. Berg may also refer to 'hill' or even to 'bear', so the Barghest is a town, hill or bear ghost. Just to make things more complicated, Barghest is also referred to as the Boguest, Boggart and Bahrgeist depending on who is describing it. Interestingly, Bahrgeist (the spelling Sir Walter Scott used in his novel *The Betrothed*) is German for 'spirit of the funeral bier', another chilling association with death.

ADDRESS Appletreewick, North Yorkshire, BD23 6DE, www.yorkshiredales.org.uk, romantics.unroll.glassware **TIP** If the Barghest hasn't got you, a visit to Parcevall Hall Gardens should be next on your list of things to do that day. There's even a tea room if you need a hot drink and a tasty treat (parcevallhallgardens.co.uk).

99 The Weather Stone

Fairly accurate forecast

The Met Office has a cutting-edge supercomputer that ingests more than 50 billion weather observations every single day. The resulting 200 terabytes of data is analysed and assessed by the mighty mechanical marvel so that the UK's weather can be forecast with astonishing precision. However, they needn't have gone to all that bother. The inhabitants of Kettlewell use the (far cheaper) Weather Stone for all their meteorological needs. And this singular silicon sensation is *never* wrong.

The Weather Stone hangs by a chain from a tree. At first glance it is difficult to see how the stone could be in any way useful. Fortunately, some obliging soul has created a comprehensive but easy-to-understand information board. Helpfully, this has also been attached to the tree, adjacent to the Weather Stone. To benefit fully from the stone's awesome predictive powers, look carefully at it and note its condition. Is it moving, for example? Take your time and don't rush this appraisal, however. At this stage you don't want to make a mistake and find it necessary to start the exercise all over again. Once you're satisfied, move your gaze to the information board. Read down the list until you find the description that best matches your experience of the Weather Stone. That will then give you an amazingly accurate assessment of the current climatic conditions. When the weather is changeable (which isn't unusual in the Dales), simply repeat the process throughout the day.

Extreme weather is fortunately rare in the Yorkshire Dales but occasionally nature does turn nasty. On the evening of 30 July, 2019, freakishly heavy rain caused extensive flooding in Swaledale, Wensleydale and Arkengarthdale. In total, 12 bridges were washed away including Grinton Bridge, as well as two miles of footpaths and bridleways wrecked. A landslip also resulted in the closure of the Settle–Carlisle railway for a time.

ADDRESS Far Lane, Kettlewell, North Yorkshire, BD23 5QU, amplified.bonkers.clinking TIP Kettlewell boasts three inns – the Blue Bell Inn, the Racehorses Hotel and The King's Head – so if the weather doesn't play ball you could always go for a pint.

100 Snaizeholme

Russet rodent refuge

Victorian banker Thomas V. Brocklehurst has a lot to answer for. In 1876 he released a pair of pet grey squirrels into Henbury Park in Cheshire. Thomas had acquired the animals in the USA during a business trip. Foolishly, he set the squirrels free because he was bored with them. Unfortunately, he wasn't the only person indulging in such reckless behaviour. Other contemporary travellers returning from North America also brought home greys that either escaped or were deliberately released into the wild.

What was not realised until much later was how devastating this would prove for Britain's native red squirrel. Greys are larger than reds and outcompete them for resources such as food. Greys also carry squirrel pox, which does not affect them but is deadly to reds. Over the course of the 20th century, red squirrel numbers declined to such a degree that they are now considered an endangered species in England and Wales.

Happily, there are pockets across the country where reds are relatively safe. Thanks to Hugh and Jane Kemp, one such haven is the Widdale Red Squirrel Reserve. The couple originally planned to cultivate Christmas trees on the land surrounding their farm at Mirk Pot in Snaizeholme. Not long afterwards red squirrels made their home in the plantation due to the plentiful food supply. The woodland, surrounded by open moorland, is essentially an island and so the reds there are naturally protected from the greys.

Red squirrels are elusive and difficult to spot in the wild. Wanting to share the experience of seeing these charismatic creatures, Hugh and Jane, in conjunction with the Yorkshire Dales National Park, have created a public viewing area. A two-and-a-half-mile-long circular trail leads to the spot, where nut-filled squirrel feeders increase the chance of seeing reds. Though as these are not tame animals, this is not something you can bank on.

ADDRESS Snaizeholme Red Squirrel Sanctuary, Hawes, North Yorkshire, DL8 3NB, www.yorkshiredales.org.uk, ambushes.sketch.sideburns **TIP** Take a walk through Cleatop Wood near Settle, a small but important area of Britain's depleted ancient woodland.

101 The Corpse Way

Stop for a rest

It's hard to imagine a time without good roads and motorised transport. But this is a world that existed not that long ago relatively speaking. Many villages in the Yorkshire Dales were isolated and remote, particularly in places such as Upper Swaledale. And not being able to hop into a car or get on a bus meant that things we take for granted now were knotty logistical problems back then.

In medieval Britain it was essential – for the sake of their eternal souls – that the recently deceased were buried in the sanctified grounds of a churchyard. Unfortunately, this was a problem for the folk who lived in Keld, for the village lacked a church. Inconveniently, the nearest place of worship was St Andrew's in Grinton, a good 16 miles to the east. And hiring a horse and cart was expensive and usually out of the question too. What to do?

The solution – a hard but practical one – was to carry the dead on foot. This led to the creation of the Corpse Way, a black but accurate name for the path between Upper Swaledale and Grinton. Our ancestors were not stupid, however. Coffins were made of lightweight wicker rather than heavy wood. And pallbearers would also stop for frequent (and much-needed) rest too. The long flat stones still found along the route are referred to locally as 'coffin stones' for good reason: it's where the coffins were carefully laid during the break in the journey. The route also carefully avoided other villages and settlements. This was to prevent the spirit of the dead from being tempted to return. Despite all these thoughtful touches, the task can never have been easy. In winter, with deep snow on the ground, it must have been a grim slog.

The Corpse Way fell out of use in 1580 when the church of St Mary the Virgin was built in Muker. Now the route has been repurposed by the Yorkshire Dales National Park as wonderfully scenic circular walk between Muker and Keld.

START/END POINT Muker, North Yorkshire, DL11 6QG, www.yorkshiredales.org.uk, dividing.envoy.mend **DISTANCE** Five and a half miles **MAP** OS 1:25,000 Explorer OL30 Yorkshire Dales – Northern & Central Areas **BEST TIME TO VISIT** Spring and summer **DIFFICULTY** A long and often strenuous walk with steep climbs and descents **TIP** The Old School Art Gallery and Craft Centre is a great place to see the work of local artists who are all inspired by the landscapes and wildlife of the Dales (www.theoldschoolmuker.co.uk).

102 Great Asby Scar

Rock, stones and fifty years on the throne

Great Asby Scar is a gem at the north-western corner of the Yorkshire Dales National Park (and is confusingly in Cumbria). The landscape is dominated by huge swathes of limestone pavement. This rocky terrain is home to plant species such as blue moor-grass and matgrass, as well as rare species of ferns that grow in the grykes (or gaps) between the limestone blocks. The scar has been granted SSSI status and is also a National Nature Reserve.

All Saints Church in Orton is an eclectic mix of architectural styles. The earliest parts of the church date from the 12th century; the splendid white castellated tower was built in the 16th century; and the porch was built in 1607. The Lancastrian architects Paley and Austin restored the chancel and north aisle in 1878.

The Beacon Monument on Monument Hill marks the spot where a beacon was lit on 21 June, 1887, to celebrate Queen Victoria's Golden Jubilee. This was one of thousands of beacons lit across the nation that day, creating a right royal tradition that was repeated in 2012 and 2022 for Queen Elizabeth II's Diamond and Platinum Jubilees respectively. It's not hard to see why the spot was selected in 1887 for there are splendid views of the Howgills to the south and of the Lake District in the west.

East of Orton is Gameland Stone Circle. This has the distinction of being one of the largest stone circles in Cumbria. It is also curiously overlooked. This may be because the stones barely rise more than a few feet in height. It's believed that they were buried or deliberately destroyed with gunpowder in the 1860s prior to the field being ploughed. A description in the *History of Westmorland and Cumberland*, published in 1777, also mentions a tumulus 'near 100 yards in circumference, rising gradually from the extremity to about the height of three yards in the middle'. This impressive monument is now sadly long gone.

START/END POINT Front Street, Orton, Penrith, Cumbria, CA10 3RJ, www.yorkshiredales.org.uk, proper.kidney.proper DISTANCE Four and a half miles MAP OS 1:25,000 Explorer OL19 Howgill Fells & Upper Eden Valley BEST TIME TO VISIT Spring and summer DIFFICULTY An occasionally challenging walk TIP Buy local produce on the second Saturday in the month at Orton Farmers' Market (www.ortonfarmers.co.uk).

103 Grimwith Reservoir

Unnatural natural beauty

The larger a town or city grows, the more difficult it can be to keep everyone living there fed and watered. Bradford faced this knotty problem as it rapidly expanded in size over the first half of the 19th century. The solution proposed by the Bradford Corporation was the creation of 11 reservoirs in the Yorkshire Dales, one of which was Grimwith (pronounced Grim'ath).

After nearly a decade of planning and construction, Grimwith Reservoir was operational by 1864. One necessary sacrifice was the loss of the hamlets of Grimwith and Gate Up, which were engulfed when the reservoir was filled. A comprehensive report in the *Bradford Observer* on 26 May, 1864, stated that the new reservoir could hold '634,000,000 gallons' of water and had 'been full, and nearly full since last autumn'. This was not the last word on Grimwith, however. Work began to increase the size of the reservoir in 1976. Seven years and a lot of toil and effort later, Grimwith was seven times larger and the water level raised by 66 feet.

One important structure thankfully not lost to the waters of Grimwith is a rare 16th-century cruck-built barn, known as High Laithe (laithe being the Viking word for barn). A cruck barn is constructed around huge A-shaped frames, known as crucks. This makes High Laithe very different in shape from the stone barns more commonly found across the Dales. It's thought that the large trees needed to make cruck barns became scarce in the 17th century and so barn designs changed after this. High Laithe was moved when Grimwith was altered in the 1970s and can now be found at the south-eastern corner of the reservoir.

Although Grimwith is artificial it still attracts a wide variety of wildfowl. Take a walk around its banks and – depending on the time of year – you're likely to see birds such as greylag and Canada geese, as well as curlew, lapwings and sedge warblers.

START/END POINT Grimwith Reservoir, Hebden, North Yorkshire, BD23 5ED, www.yorkshirewater.com, prominent.blazers.void DISTANCE Four and a half miles MAP OS 1:25,000 Explorer 298 Nidderdale BEST TIME TO VISIT Spring and summer DIFFICULTY A long but relatively easy walk with no steep climbs TIP Nearby Gouthwaite Reservoir is a nature reserve and SSSI where you can see a wide range of waterfowl such as pochard and Canada geese (nidderdale-nl.org.uk).

104 Ingleton Waterfalls Trail

Watery woodland wonder

Visiting tourist attractions in the Yorkshire Dales is not a new phenomenon by any means. Take the Ingleton Waterfalls Trail, for instance. This popular walk welcomed its first paying visitors on 11 April, 1885. For the very reasonable price of 2d, happy sightseers could spend a day wandering along the trail, looking at the wonderful waterfalls along the way. Visitors soon came in their thousands from nearby industrial towns such as Bradford and Leeds.

In September 1885, the London and North-Western Railway Company ran their first excursions to Ingleton from Manchester. A reporter for the *Manchester Courier* wrote about one such trip day and noted that the place 'was so charming in variety and romantic beauty', that he was at a loss 'why such magnificent scenery as that in the neighbourhood of Ingleton is not better known'.

The woodland trail follows the course of two rivers: the Twiss (which has its source in Kingsdale) and the Doe (which rises in Chapel-le-Dale). The two rivers meet in Ingleton where they become the river Greta, a tributary of the Lune in Lancaster.

It's on the Twiss section of the walk that you can see the utterly charming divided form of Pecca Falls, Hollybush Spout and the 45-foot-tall Thornton Force, which plunges over an impressive limestone cliff. Thanks to ever-grinding geological processes, Thornton Force has moved some 165 feet back from its original post-glacial position 17,000 years ago.

The waterfalls on the Doe stretch of the trail are different in character but no less interesting. Beezley Falls are a series of drops that eventually splits three ways. The two drops that make up Rival Falls are at either end of the 'Black Hole', a plunge pool said to be more than 80 feet deep. Finally, there is Snow Falls, which is large but can be frustratingly tricky to see due to overhanging trees.

START/END POINT Broadwood, Ingleton, North Yorkshire, LA6 3FT, www.ingletonwaterfallstrail.co.uk, centuries.shorter.forgives **DISTANCE** Four and a half miles **MAP** OS 1:25,000 Explorer OL02 Yorkshire Dales – Southern & Western Areas **BEST TIME TO VISIT** Any time of year, though the woodland in autumn is particularly beautiful **DIFFICULTY** Strenuous in places **TIP** Enjoy the relaxing ambience of the Game Cock Inn, a traditional pub at the heart of the village of Austwick (www.gamecockinn.co.uk).

105 Kettlewell

Walk along the Wharfe

The village of Kettlewell is nestled right on the banks of the river Wharfe. Therefore, it should be no surprise that the name Kettlewell is probably derived from the Anglo-Saxon *Chetelewelle*, which refers to a spring or stream in a deep valley. It's under this name that Kettlewell is recorded in the Domesday Book in 1086.

Kettlewell is a location well used in TV and film productions. Steve Coogan filmed a (rather rude) song and dance sequence on the streets of Kettlewell for the 2010 movie *The Trip*. And the village was transformed into the fictional Knapley in 2003 for *Calendar Girls*, starring Helen Mirren, Penelope Wilton and Julie Walters. And (naturally) Kettlewell has been used in both the original and modern versions of *All Creatures Great and Small.*

St Mary's Church in Kettlewell dates from the early 19th century though it stands on the site of a much older structure. The original church was built in 1120 by the de Arches, a Norman family who owned the village at this time. The only thing that remains of the older church is the simple but striking tub-shaped font.

The river Wharfe starts its journey at the meeting of Oughtershaw Beck and Green Field Beck in Langstrothdale. Wharfedale, the dale through which the river flows, has long been noted for its natural splendour. An advert in the *Newcastle Chronicle* in 1768 noted that Wharfedale is one of 'the most fertile and pleasant Vales in Yorkshire, up on the river Wharfe, which is well stocked with fish'. The Wharfe can be unpredictable, however. Heavy rain on the fells can cause flooding in the dale. In August 1880, the *Lancaster Gazette* reported that a severe storm caused problems in the neighbourhood of Kettlewell and Buckden. After several days of rain the Wharfe had risen 'two feet almost instantaneously', and that 'some calves and sheep were taken down the stream, and a considerable quantity of hay was carried away'.

START/END POINT Kettlewell, North Yorkshire, BD23 5QZ, www.yorkshiredales.org.uk, outhouse.pine.laptop DISTANCE Four miles MAP OS 1:25,000 Explorer OL30 Yorkshire Dales – Northern & Central Areas BEST TIME TO VISIT Any time of year DIFFICULTY A moderate walk with some steep sections TIP Have a refreshing hot or cold drink and a bite to eat at the &then… Tasting Deli in Kettlewell.

106 Malham Tarn

Walk at a glacial pace

The last Ice Age left its mark on the Yorkshire Dales. The largest and most distinctive of those relics is Malham Tarn, which formed some 10,000 years ago when a depression in the landscape was filled by melting glacial ice-water. Impressive though Malham Tarn is, it was once far, far larger. The accumulation of silt over the millennia halved the size of the tarn, creating the boggy area on its western shore known as Tarn Moss.

There are relatively few lakes in the Yorkshire Dales and this is because limestone – the rock that underlies the region – is porous. This means that water dribbles away over time rather like a leaky bath. Malham Tarn persists because it sits upon a bed of ancient slate which – unlike limestone – is impermeable.

Tarn Moss is a national nature reserve, though don't go there expecting exotic flora and fauna. The soggy landscape is poor in nutrients and slightly acidic. It is also ombrotrophic, which denotes that an area is 'rain fed'. This means that whatever water or nutrients are found there are derived almost entirely from rain or snow. For this reason, Tarn Moss is dominated by vegetation that thrives in this sort of environment, such as mosses and bog asphodel.

Tarn House overlooks the northern end of Malham Tarn. The property was built late in the 18th century for Thomas Lister, Lord Ribblesdale, though it was initially called Malham Water House. It came into the possession of James Morrison in 1852 and was eventually inherited by Morrison's son, Walter. It was during Walter's ownership that Charles Kingsley came to visit. It's thought that Kingsley was inspired to write his classic novel *The Water-Babies* during his stay at Tarn House. Walter Morrison was twice the Liberal Unionist MP for Skipton, and was a notable donor to the Palestine Exploration Fund. Tarn House was gifted to the National Trust in 1946.

START/END POINT Malham Moor, North Yorkshire, BD24 9PT, www.nationaltrust.org.uk, chickens.shirtless.flips DISTANCE About four and a quarter miles MAP OS 1:25,000 Explorer OL02 Yorkshire Dales – Southern & Western Areas BEST TIME TO VISIT Any time of year DIFFICULTY A challenging walk, though the shorter route around Tarn Moss is easier TIP The Dry Valley of the Watlowes, south of Malham Tarn, was also formed by a glacier though – as the name suggests – no water runs through it now.

107 The Norber Erratics

Rock tour

During the various ice ages of the past 100,000 years, large swathes of the British Isles were covered by thick ice sheets and glaciers. These frosty formations shaped the land, carving out valleys and whittling mountains down to size. As the glaciers slowly ground across the landscape they also took rocks and boulders along for the ride. These were eventually dumped far from their starting point, often where the native rock was entirely different. This created a puzzle for early geologists, who – not knowing about ice ages – could not understand how these anomalous rocks ended up where they did. They therefore referred to these peculiar relics as erratics, from the Latin *errare*, which means 'to wander'. By far the best place to see erratics in Yorkshire is on the southern slopes of Ingleborough near the village of Austwick. Known as the Norber erratics, the rocks are great chunks of greywacke sandstone ripped from beds laid down during the Silurian period. Many of the erratics are balanced on small pedestals of limestone almost as though they were carefully placed there. It's thought that the erratics protected the underlying limestone from erosion whereas the surrounding limestone was gradually worn away.

The Norber erratics bear the scars of their time spent trapped in ice. Look carefully at the rocks and you may see parallel grooves and scratches on the surface. These were caused by particles of grit in the glacier rubbing along the rock and leaving a permanent mark.

There are no glaciers in Yorkshire now and there haven't been since the last ice age ended roughly 10,000 years ago. The Norber erratics were probably deposited around that time, when the onset of a warmer climate caused the ice sheets to melt. It was this change in the climate that also allowed a clever ape named *Homo sapiens* – us, in other words – to make a bid for glory, conquer the world and to take notice of rocks that were curiously out of place.

START/END POINT Yorkshire Dales National Park car park, Clapham, North Yorkshire, LA2 8EQ, nosedive.masts.finalists **DISTANCE** About five miles **MAP** OS 1:25,000 Explorer OL02 Yorkshire Dales – Southern & Western Areas **BEST TIME TO VISIT** Any time of year, though winter (when the sun is lower in the sky) is particularly dramatic **DIFFICULTY** A steep climb to reach Thwaite Lane and then up on to Norber **TIP** The strangely proportioned St James' Church in Clapham was originally constructed in the 15th century and then extensively rebuilt in the nineteenth.

108 Old Gang

Heavy Metal

Lead is a curious metal. It is very dense and yet it is extremely malleable. It is resistant to corrosion and has a remarkably low melting point of just 327 degrees Celsius. Lead is also incredibly useful and can be found in car batteries, electronics, and on roofs, where it is used to seal joints to form a watertight seal. However, lead has a darkly sinister side too. It is a *really* bad idea to ingest lead in even the smallest of doses. Health problems caused by lead include (but are not limited to) damage to the brain and kidneys, anaemia, depression and decreased libido. It is for these reasons that lead is no longer used to make water pipes or to make white paint whiter. Lead was once plentiful in the hills of the North Pennines, including the Yorkshire Dales. In the 18th and 19th centuries numerous mines opened across the Dales, particularly in Swaledale. If you know what to look for, you can still see the remains of spoil heaps dotted across the landscape. More obvious are the ruins of buildings associated with the lead industry; the largest and most impressive of which is the Old Gang Smelting Mill.

The mill was probably built in 1846, though strangely there are no records of its exact date of construction. The mill served the nearby Old Gang Mine and was used to process lead ore – known as galena – into pure lead ingots. The most striking aspect of the Old Gang mill is the solidly square chimney, which towers over the rest of the complex. The mill's furnace was fired using peat as fuel. To the west of the mill are the remains of the peat store. The store was 390 feet long and 20 feet wide, and was once said to hold three years' worth of peat, which was cut from the hills nearby.

Old Gang had a short working life. The price of lead dropped in the late 19th century due to increased foreign competition. Swaledale's mines couldn't compete and so the industry declined. Old Gang limped on until 1913 when it closed for good.

START/END POINT High Lane, Kearton, North Yorkshire, DL11 6PW, www.yorkshiredales.org.uk, royal.shameless.tuck **DISTANCE** About two miles (or five and a half for a longer circular walk) **MAP** OS 1:25,000 Explorer OL30 Yorkshire Dales – Northern & Central Areas **BEST TIME TO VISIT** Any time of year **DIFFICULTY** The linear walk along the road is easy **TIP** Surrender Bridge was used in the opening credits of the BBC's adaptation of *All Creatures Great and Small*.

109 Reeth

Have a Swale of a time

The village of Reeth had its beginnings in the Iron Age, at least 2,500 years ago. And it's not hard to see why our ancient ancestors decided that it was a good location for a settlement. Reeth is north of the river Swale, just above a flood plain, and is protected on its eastern edge by Arkle Beck. The name is thought to derive from the Old English for 'rough place'. Reeth is mentioned in the Domesday Book. The tenant-in-chief was Count Alan (of Brittany), though what benefits he enjoyed are unclear. Reeth was described as 'waste', which means that it may have been destroyed by William the Conqueror in his brutal act of revenge known as the 'Harrying of the North'. Happily, Reeth has more than recovered in the centuries since and is now a thriving and popular place to live or to visit.

Village life was dominated by the lead mining industry in the 18th and 19th centuries. This provided an occasionally precarious living for locals. During financial downturns many miners relied on the original parish workhouse in Reeth, built in 1753 on Back Lane. This was replaced in the 1840s when an old mansion was purchased for £700 and converted into a workhouse to house 60 inmates. The building is now home to the Copper Kettle tearoom.

Reeth is the focus point for the wonderful Swaledale Festival. This 15-day celebration of local creativity has been running annually since 1972. Events are held at venues in Swaledale, Wensleydale and Arkengarthdale in chapels, village halls and art centres. Performers who have taken part include the Black Dyke Band, Kathryn Tickell and the Poet Laureate, Simon Armitage.

Reeth is overlooked by Low Common, a patchwork of fields below Fremington Edge. The common is the quintessential Dales landscape, attractively crisscrossed with drystone walls and dotted with traditional stone barns.

START/END POINT Silver Street, Reeth, North Yorkshire, DL11 6SP, www.yorkshiredales.org.uk, ticket.surfacing.passages DISTANCE About two and a half miles MAP OS 1:25,000 Explorer OL30 Yorkshire Dales – Northern & Central Areas BEST TIME TO VISIT Late summer when the heather is in bloom is particularly rewarding DIFFICULTY Reasonably straightforward though some walking on uneven ground TIP Learn more about the region at the wonderfully comprehensive Swaledale Museum (www.swaledalemuseum.org).

110 The Shawl

Wrap up well

The Shawl is a public footpath that strikes out westwards from Leyburn. The view is splendid all year round and a fine place to be when the sun is out and you need to gently stretch your legs. In June 1900 it was described in the *Northern Weekly Gazette* as 'the greatest attraction of Wensleydale'. A century and a quarter on, that's still a reasonable if obviously subjective assessment.

The origin of the name is obscure. The most likely explanation is that it derives from 'shaw', meaning a wood, or possibly from the Old Norse *schalle* or *skali*, meaning huts or shelters. The more romantic incline to a legend involving Mary, Queen of Scots.

Mary Stuart was born in 1542, the daughter of James V of Scotland and Mary of Guise. She inherited the Scottish throne six days after she was born when James died from cholera (or possibly dysentery). Various regents ruled in Mary's name while she was brought up in France. To describe her life as eventful is an understatement. She was married three times. Her first husband, Francis II of France died two years after they were wed. Mary's second husband, Lord Darnley, was found murdered and his residence destroyed in an explosion. Her third husband, James Hepburn, was thought to have had a hand in Darnley's murder but was acquitted. And then, in July 1567, she was forced to abdicate in favour of her one-year-old son, James VI (later James I of England).

Unfortunately, she then had the very bad idea of fleeing to England and requesting help from her cousin, Elizabeth I. Elizabeth was nervous of Mary as some thought that Mary had a more legitimate claim to the English throne. Elizabeth responded by confining Mary to a number of castles and stately homes, including nearby Bolton Castle. According to the legend, Mary escaped from there and fled towards Leyburn. In her panic she dropped her shawl, and the footpath was named after this (unlikely) event.

START/END POINT Leyburn Shawl, Leyburn, North Yorkshire, DL8 5DG, www.welcometoleyburn.co.uk, addicted.professed.nerve DISTANCE About four and a half miles MAP OS 1:25,000 Explorer OL30 Yorkshire Dales – Northern & Central Areas BEST TIME TO VISIT Any time of year DIFFICULTY Reasonably easy with no steep climbs TIP If you have a sweet tooth then you *definitely* need to visit Inspired Chocolate when visiting Leyburn (www.inspiredchocolate.co.uk).

111 Staveley Nature Reserve

For the birds

Staveley has long had a reputation as a special place for those interested in nature. In 1782, the third edition of Ely Hargrove's classic *The History of the Castle, Town, and Forest of Knaresborough* was published. In a chapter snappily entitled 'An Account of the Most Curious Plants and Shrubs in the Neighbourhood of Knaresborough', Hargrove noted a variety of plants that had been spotted growing in and around what was then wetland known as Staveley Carrs. These included water violets, smallage (wild celery), yellow water lily and marsh horsetail.

Staveley Carrs was drained to grow crops in the 19th century and then quarried for aggregates such as sand and gravel in the 20th. The quarries were worked out by the 1970s creating an opportunity to do something constructive with the land. The neatly circular solution was to flood the quarries and try to reinstate the original wetland landscape. After 30 years of naturalisation, the site was acquired by the Yorkshire Wildlife Trust in 2002. The trust have been the custodians of the reserve ever since.

The nature reserve is 79 hectares in size and includes the two flooded quarries, grassland and woodland. This variety has created a space for wildlife to thrive. Over 200 different species have been recorded at Staveley, including such charismatic creatures as otters and barn owls. The bird species to look for is the water rail, a permanent resident at Staveley. Although relatively common, the water rail is a secretive bird that is more likely to be heard than seen. The rail looks not dissimilar to a moorhen, though it has a smaller, more flattened body that allows it to thread its way through reedbeds. The wetland habitat is also home to a variety of species of dragonfly. These insects are highly efficient predators that prey on other flies, bees and even butterflies. They are superb fliers, agile and fast – they have been recorded as flying at 30 miles an hour.

START/END POINT Staveley Nature Reserve, Minskip Road, Boroughbridge, North Yorkshire, HG5 9LQ, www.ywt.org.uk, spoons.dose.bogus DISTANCE There are various routes around the site MAP OS 1:25,000 Explorer 299 Ripon & Boroughbridge BEST TIME TO VISIT Any time of year, though winter is good for migratory birds DIFFICULTY Largely flat with good paths TIP Nearby Burton Leonard Lime Quarries is another reclaimed industrial landscape that is now a haven for wildlife (www.ywt.org.uk).

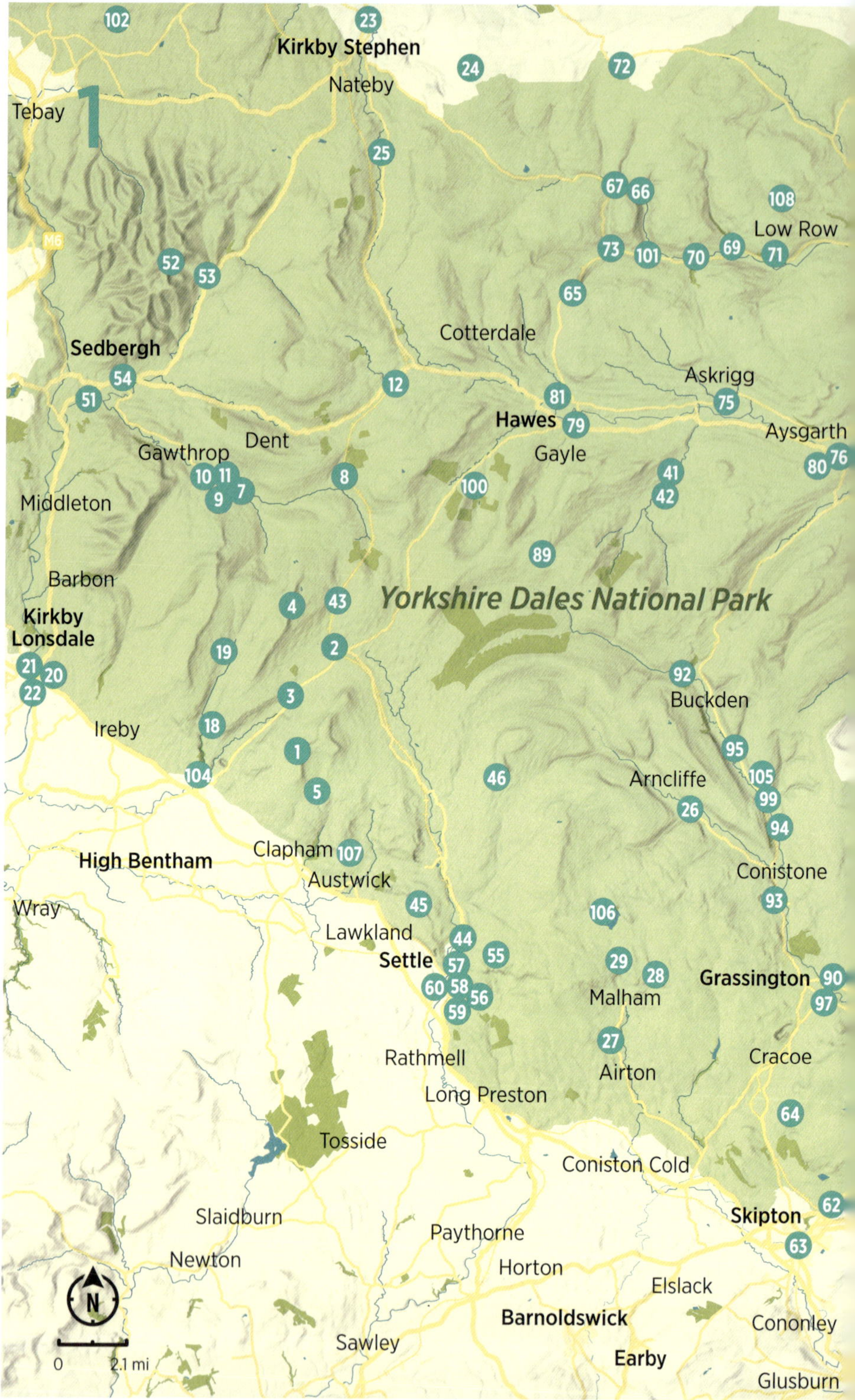
1
Kirkby Stephen
Nateby
Tebay
M6
Sedbergh
Cotterdale
Low Row
Askrigg
Hawes
Aysgarth
Gayle
Dent
Gawthrop
Middleton
Barbon
Kirkby Lonsdale
Yorkshire Dales National Park
Buckden
Ireby
Arncliffe
Conistone
Clapham
Austwick
High Bentham
Wray
Lawkland
Settle
Grassington
Malham
Rathmell
Airton
Cracoe
Long Preston
Tosside
Coniston Cold
Slaidburn
Skipton
Paythorne
Newton
Horton
Elslack
Barnoldswick
Cononley
Sawley
Earby
Glusburn
N
0
2.1 mi
1
2
3
4
5
7
8
9
10
11
12
18
19
20
21
22
23
24
25
26
27
28
29
41
42
43
44
45
46
51
52
53
54
55
56
57
58
59
60
62
63
64
65
66
67
69
70
71
72
73
75
76
79
80
81
89
90
92
93
94
95
97
99
100
101
102
104
105
106
107
108

2
Gayles
Barton
Gilling West
Middleton Tyas
Great Smeaton
East Cowton
Richmond
A1(M)
Reeth
Marske
48
47
Scorton
68
109
Marrick
Colburn
Danby Wiske
Catterick Garrison
Tunstall
77
Northallerton
Bellerby
Hunton
Scruton
78
Leyburn
Wensley
110
87
Finghall
74
85
82
Middleham
86
84
River Swale
Bedale
6
Carlton
83
Burneston
Pickhill
Masham
Swinton
31
A1(M)
30
Mickley
Wath
Rainton
Lofthouse
34
RIPON
Dishforth
50
49
33
Borough-bridge
Pateley Bridge
Bishop Monkton
35
Low Laithe
Minskip
103
36
32
38
37
111
88
91
98
Burnsall
Appletreewick
Ripley
Darley
Birstwith
Knaresborough
Harrogate
Bolton Abbey
14
13
61
96
Beckwithshaw
Timble
Addingham
15
Ilkley
Stainburn
Huby
Wetherby
17
16
Otley
A1(M)
40
39
Harewood

Ed Glinert, David Taylor
111 Places in Yorkshire
That You Shouldn't Miss
ISBN 978-3-7408-1167-9

David Taylor
111 Places in Northumberland
That You Shouldn't Miss
ISBN 978-3-7408-2923-0

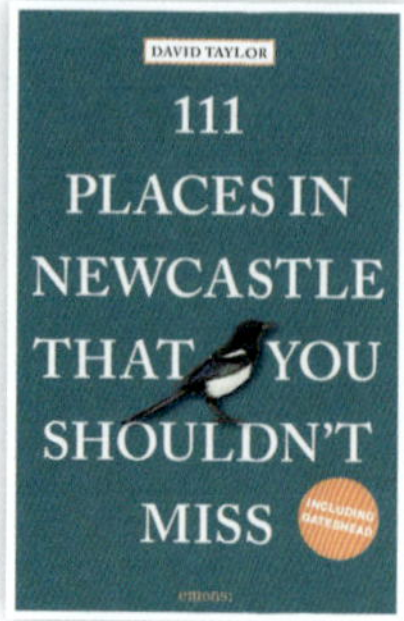

David Taylor
111 Places in Newcastle
That You Shouldn't Miss
ISBN 978-3-7408-1043-6

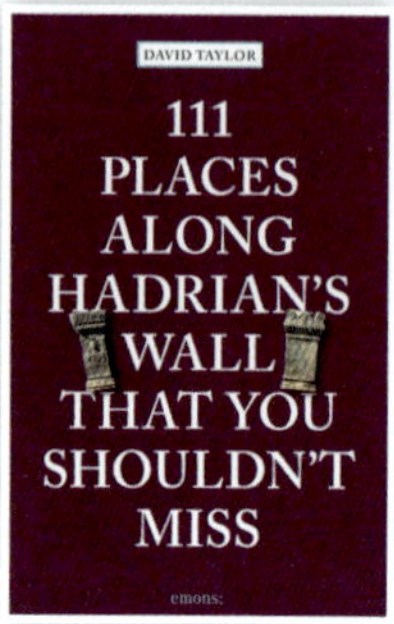

David Taylor
111 Places along Hadrian's Wall
That You Shouldn't Miss
ISBN 978-3-7408-1425-0

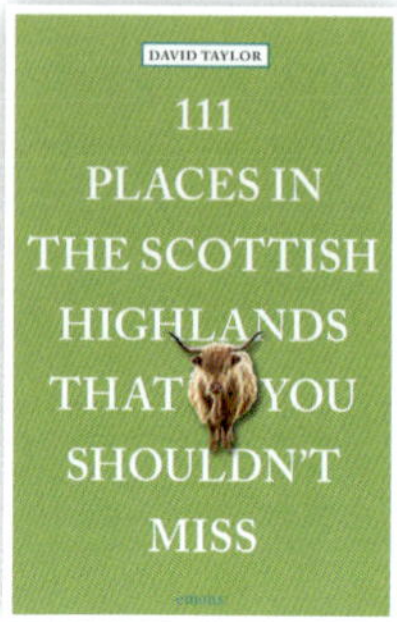

David Taylor
111 Places in the Scottish High-
lands That You Shouldn't Miss
ISBN 978-3-7408-2064-0

Solange Berchemin
111 Places in the Lake District
That You Shouldn't Miss
ISBN 978-3-7408-2824-0

Roly Smith, Chris Gilbert
111 Places in the Peak District
That You Shouldn't Miss
ISBN 978-3-7408-2551-5

Ed Glinert, David Taylor
111 Places in Oxford
That You Shouldn't Miss
ISBN 978-3-7408-1990-3

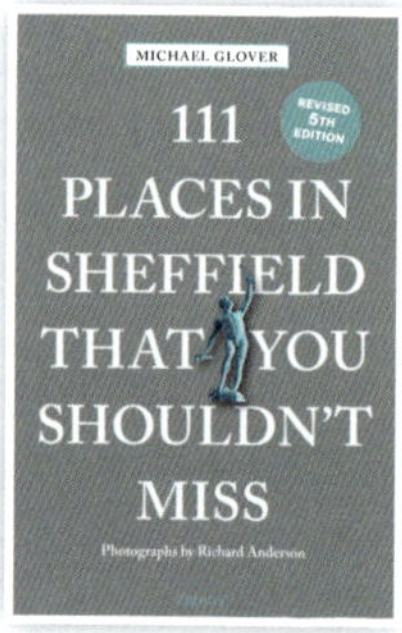

Michael Glover, Richard Anderson
111 Places in Sheffield
That You Shouldn't Miss
ISBN 978-3-7408-2348-1

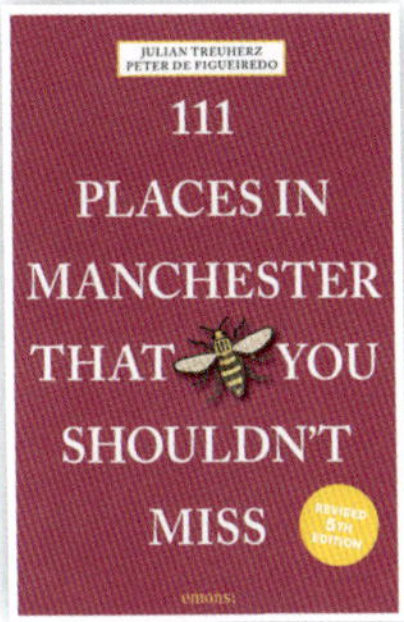

Julian Treuherz,
Peter de Figueiredo
111 Places in Manchester
That You Shouldn't Miss
ISBN 978-3-7408-2645-1

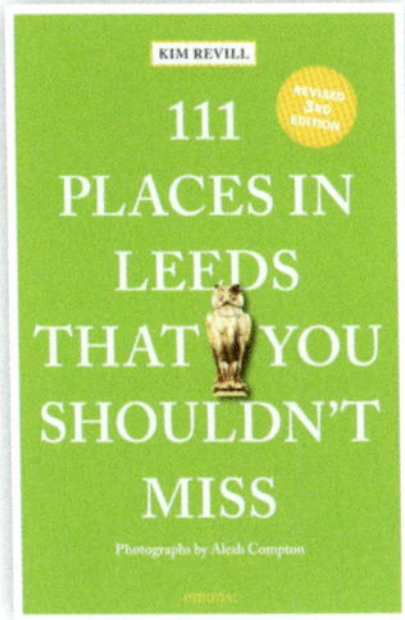

Kim Revill, Alesh Compton
111 Places in Leeds
That You Shouldn't Miss
ISBN 978-3-7408-2059-6

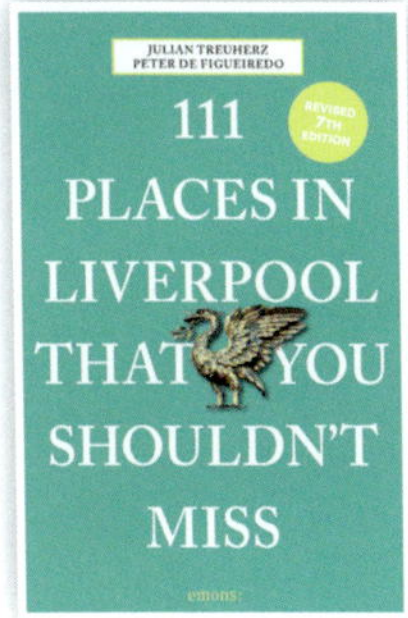

Julian Treuherz,
Peter de Figueiredo
111 Places in Liverpool
That You Shouldn't Miss
ISBN 978-3-7408-2515-7

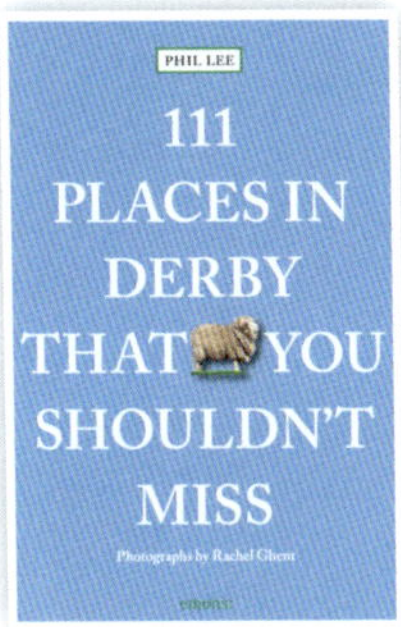

Phil Lee, Rachel Ghent
111 Places in Derby
That You Shouldn't Miss
ISBN 978-3-7408-2432-7

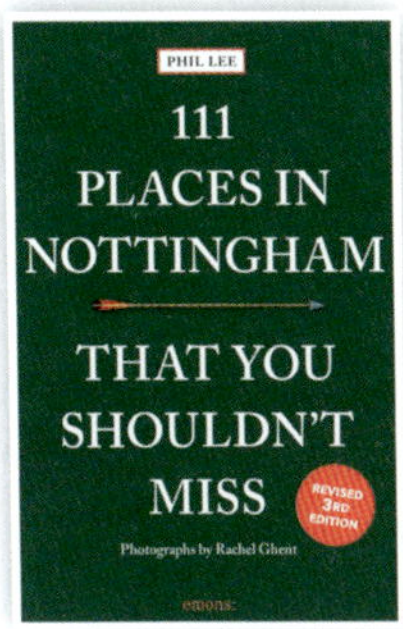

Phil Lee, Rachel Ghent
111 Places in Nottingham
That You Shouldn't Miss
ISBN 978-3-7408-2925-4

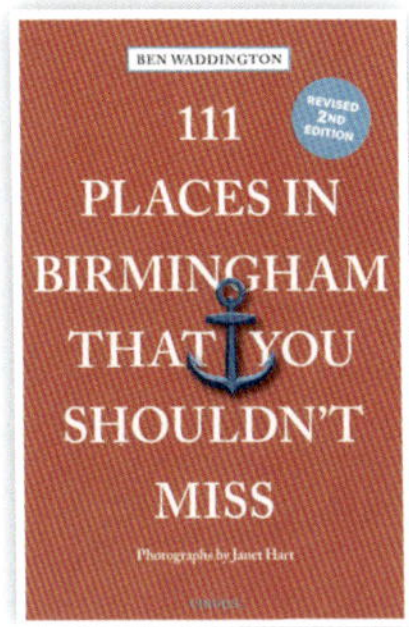

Ben Waddington, Janet Hart
111 Places in Birmingham
That You Shouldn't Miss
ISBN 978-3-7408-2200-2

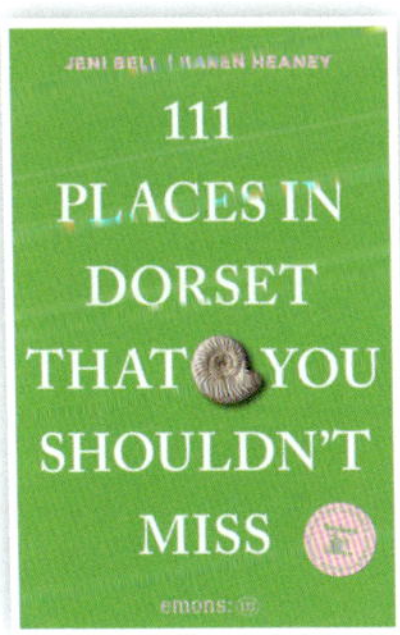

Karen Heaney, Jeni Bell
111 Places in Dorset
That You Shouldn't Miss
ISBN 978-3-7408-3018-2

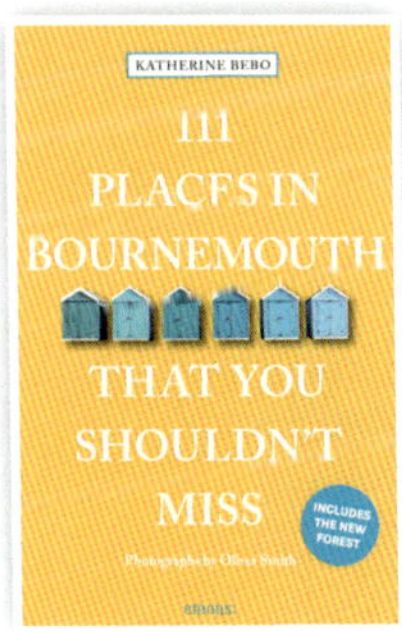

Katherine Bebo, Oliver Smith
111 Places in Bournemouth
That You Shouldn't Miss
ISBN 978-3-7408-2646-8

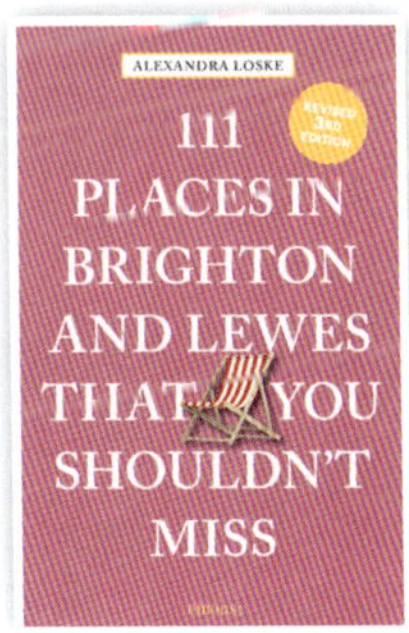

Alexandra Loske
111 Places in Brighton and
Lewes That You Shouldn't Miss
ISBN 978-3-7408-1727-5

ACKNOWLEDGEMENTS

This book couldn't have been written without the assistance of some *very* good-natured people. For their help, I'd like to thank Jacqueline Naylor at Bolton Castle; Jade and the staff at Billy Bob's Parlour; Patrick Smith and the players at Skipton Little Theatre; Dani and Nertil at Caffé Lago di Como; the Revd Sue McWhinney, Associate Priest, St Michael the Archangel in Kirkby-in-Malhamdale; Toby and Jane Whittaker at Whittaker's Distillery; Michael Kusz (and Joe the Crow) of Graculus Sculptures; Josie Guthrie at Settle Victoria Hall; Alex Samuel at Ilkley Toy Museum; Marie Batty, Kirkby Lonsdale's Town Information Manager; Anna Burdon at Jervaulx Abbey; Mark Thompson at Hardraw Force Waterfall; Mark Sproat at the Churches Conservation Trust; Andrew Fagg at the Yorkshire Dales National Park Authority; Oliver and Paul at Stump Cross Caverns; Sasha Jackson-Brown at the Himalayan Garden; Moira Smith and Bernard Chyzy at Bolton Abbey; Rob Shaw at Embsay & Bolton Abbey Steam Railway; Carolyn Smith at Ripon Museums; Craig Buckton at The Forbidden Corner; Hannah at The Oldest Sweet Shop In The World; and Steve Amphlett and the Settle Flowerpot Festival organisers.

I also benefitted hugely from the support of Laura Olk at Emons Verlag and Ros Horton of Cambridge Editorial, for which thank you! The biggest thank you, however, goes to my wife Tania, who has shared in many of my adventures in the Yorkshire Dales.

NOTES

Most of the places in this book are easily found. For more obscure locations use the What3Words app (available for iOS and Android) or website. To navigate to a place, type the three words found in the address section (exactly as shown) into What3Words. Then click or tap on 'Navigate' and select your preferred mapping app to see the route to the place from your current location. That said, although mobile phones are a useful tool, a good map and compass is preferable in so many ways – the Ordnance Survey 1:25,000 Explorer maps for the region are excellent and provide a wealth of useful detail. And also consider attending a mountain navigation course before heading out into the hills for the first time too.

The Yorkshire Dales National Park website (www.yorkshiredales.org.uk) is a wonderful resource for further information about the area covered in the book. There are maps and route descriptions for many of the walks mentioned in this book both on the website and on the Yorkshire Dales app. Another *very* useful website when planning a trip to the Dales is that of the Nidderdale National Landscape (www.nidderdale-nl.org.uk).

THE AUTHOR

David Taylor is a professional freelance landscape photographer and writer who lives in Northumberland. His first camera was a Kodak Instamatic. Since then, he's used every type of camera imaginable: from bulky 4x5 film cameras to pocket-sized digital compacts. David has written over 40 books, as well as supplying images and articles to both regional and national magazines. When David is not outdoors he can be found at home with his wife and an increasingly large number of tripods.
www.davidtaylorphotography.co.uk